THE LITTLE ARMAGEDDON

The Great Controversy Within the Seventh-day Adventist Church

John Churchill
with Dwight Turner

A Lay Minister's Response to the Shepherd's Rod Offshoot Problem Within the Seventh-day Adventist Church.

Order this book online at www.trafford.com
or email orders@trafford.com

Most Trafford titles are also available at major online book retailers.

© Copyright 2010 John Churchill.
All rights reserved. No part of this publication may be reproduced, stored
in a retrieval system, or transmitted, in any form or by any means, electronic,
mechanical, photocopying, recording, or otherwise, without
the written prior permission of the author.

Printed in Victoria, BC, Canada.

ISBN: 978-1-4269-3241-0 (sc)
ISBN: 978-1-4269-3252-6 (eb)

Library of Congress Control Number: 2010905811

*Our mission is to efficiently provide the world's finest, most comprehensive
book publishing service, enabling every author to experience success.
To find out how to publish your book, your way, and have it available
worldwide, visit us online at www.trafford.com*

Trafford rev. 06/04/2010

www.trafford.com

North America & international
toll-free: 1 888 232 4444 (USA & Canada)
phone: 250 383 6864 ♦ fax: 812 355 4082

Dedication:

This book is dedicated to:

Elder David Swaby – a warrior of the cross, a faithful watchman, a leader extraordinaire.

Brother Dwight Turner – a dedicated worker in the vineyard of our Lord.

My dear mother – Joycelyn Myrna Facey (nee Hewitt) who went to sleep in Jesus, December 07, 2004.

Acknowledgment

Thanks to my dear wife and four children for allowing me the time to dedicate to the preparation of this handbook.

Thanks to Dwight Turner for his encouragement and for graciously allowing the inclusion of his article on Davidians in this book.

Thanks to Elder David Swaby for his love, care and concern and for his Christian example; for being a real spiritual father and mentor to me. Thanks also to him for not only allowing me to interview him but also permitting me to include its contents in the book.

Table of Contents

Dedication:	v
Acknowledgment	vii
Preface	xv
Chapter One Edification on the Shepherd's Rod:	
Their Story	1
Introduction and Background Reading:	1
Apostate Movements	5
A Brief History (by a Shepherd's Rod group)	6
Chapter Two Edification on the Shepherd's Rod:	
The Church's Story	9
Chapter Three Cooperation and Unity Will Help Us to	
Overcome in the Battle of the Little Armageddon!	14
Some Heat in the Little Armageddon:	
A Battle Royal!	14
Marshalling a valuable weapon through cooperation:	16
Who Are The Davidian Seventh-day Adventists?	17
Introduction	17
What Do They Believe?	19
V. T. Houteff's Hidden Agenda	21
The History of the Shepherd's Rod Movement	22
A Bold Claim by Victor Houteff	33
Houteff's Teachings Examined	33
Perfect Safety	35
When Will Christ Set Up His Kingdom	
And Rule On The Throne?	38
The New Covenant - Yet To Come or Already In	
Existence?	40
Another Subtle Heresy Taught By Houteff	42
Does The Mount of Olives Split Twice?	47

Ezekiel 9	48
Who Are The 144,000?	56
Another Teaching of Houteff Contradicted By Mrs. White	62
Fanciful Interpretations of Bible Texts	63
Conclusion	65
Author's Note:	68

Chapter Four The Importance of the Gift of Prophecy to the Battle of the Little Armageddon — 74

- Spiritual Gifts — 75
- Prophets, Prophecy and Biblical Tests for a Prophet: — 76
- False Prophets: — 79
- Spirit of Prophecy: — 81
- Visions — 82

Chapter Five Biblical Tests for a Prophet (A Study): — 89

- The Gift of Prophecy — 89
- The Prophet Daniel — 90
- The Gift of Prophecy in Bible Times — 91
- The Gift of Prophecy Beyond Bible Times — 92
- The Gift of Prophecy Today — 95

Chapter Six Preparing for the Enemy by Identifying the Enemy — 102

- Here are a Few Bible References on False Prophets and False Teachers: — 102
- The Lay Minister Says:
  How to Identify Shepherd's Rods — 104
- Strategies of the Shepherd's Rod Offshoot Group — 106
- Framework / Summary of Their Strategy — 110

Chapter Seven Confronting False Teachers — 112

- Confronting False Teachers:
  A Prescription for Action — 112
- Steps taken at the church under attack: — 113
- Their reaction: — 113
- Other Steps taken: — 114

Tips to Leaders: What to Say to the Church	115
Other Statements you could use:	118
Getting Them Out of the Church: A Surgical Prescription	118
A Template or Sample Letter	120

Chapter Eight Be Armed to the Teeth — 122

Identify Them!	122
Can their claim that they are Seventh-day Adventists be justified?	126
Membership on a Spiritual Basis	127
Baptismal Vow # 5:	130
Baptismal Vow # 7:	131
Baptismal Vow # 9:	133
Baptismal Vow # 11:	136
Baptismal Vow # 13:	138

Chapter Nine Experience Teaches Wisdom! Personal Experiences From A Veteran Warrior in the Battle of the Little Armageddon — 148

First Experience:	149
Exodus From The Church and Impact of the SR on a Young Church	149
The Elder's Response and A Massive SR Invasion	150
Sabbath School Time	151
What was special about the SR? / Twisting Ellen White's writing	152
A Very Wicked Strategy of the SR	153
Strategies of the SR Identified by the Elder	154
SR Who Came Back to the Fold?	154
Could You Know the Shepherd's Rods?	155
SR Literature Distribution Strategy	155
Do the SR Approach Non-SDA's?	156
Have Any Church Leaders Become Shepherd's Rods?	156
SR Offering to Help Members	157
Insisting on Kneeling to Pray	157

The greatest defense against the SR?	158
Should we Study Their Doctrines?	159
Mixing Truth and Error	159
What Has Kept Them Going?	159
Advice to New Converts and Others	160
Study the Word of God	160
The devil is Busy and, ready to Destroy – But Time Will Soon be Up For him	161
Interview Postscript:	163

Chapter Ten How to Develop Superior Counteracting Weapons for the Little Armageddon — **166**

Another Favourite Target	166
New Convert Preparation	167
The Need for Nurturing Churches	167
Other Ways of Attack	168
Members and Leaders Must Be Diligent	168
Provide Good Materials For Members to Study!	169
The Lure of Economic Gain	170
Be Our Brothers' Keeper	171
Share Problems	171
The True Remnant	172
Psychological Warfare!	172
Witnessing: An Absolute Necessity	174
Final Rx: PRAYER: The Ultimate Weapon!!	176
The Bee Sting	177

Chapter Eleven The Little Armageddon is not for the Weak or the Inexperienced Soldier of the Cross – Nor for the Fainthearted! — **183**

Some General Advice for Members	183
List of Don'ts	183
Final Marching Orders: A Bitter Pill – but Excellent Medicine!	186
Parting Salvo!	187
Little Armageddon no More!!!	190

The Last Thing	191
My Final Appeal	192

PREFACE

I started this particular work in about 2003 and have persevered with the task in spite of my intense caring, sharing, involvement and occupation with my family, a full time job, my local church, a many-faceted personal ministry that expanded into a family ministry and later a wider ministry that now has the majority of members being outside of my family. Additionally, I have been involved in many fortuitous preoccupations over the years. During the time, the work has experienced as much changes as a chameleon can muster! God has been good, He is good and He will always be good! Praise the Lord! I have tenaciously visited and revisited the work because I believe it is important and will help in the total scheme of things regarding the preservation and saving of souls for the Kingdom of God. If even one person is snatched from satan's clutches or prevented from falling into his trap, I believe the copious hours that were dedicated to this work would have been more than worth it! Praise the Lord!

The Shepherd's Rod group has been around for many years wreaking havoc ... havoc? Yes, havoc in the Seventh-day Adventist Church. However, in many churches (too many) this fact is not known by the general membership. In fact, in many churches not even the Elders and Leaders are aware of who the Shepherd's Rods are and what their real mission is. Hence, they are usually very accommodating of them ... and others are just totally ignorant of them, while others are just plain scared of them. The easiest way to deceive someone is to obtain their trust. The most dangerous people in this context are those that have been in the church, know the doctrines of the church and pass themselves off as Seventh-day Adventists; such is the case with many of the Shepherd's Rods; that makes them rather dangerous.

This little manual is written for all such persons and others, but especially for the Elder, Leader or Member who wants to be able to identify this offshoot group, know what to do about them and how to approach them. We know that Armageddon is coming! Simply put, that's when gog and magog (the enemies of God) will engage the Archangel Michael (Jesus Christ, God the Son) and His forces of good in a final battle. However, as that time approaches satan is going about as a roaring lion seeking whom he may devour! He is waging war right in the true Church of God! He is spreading his destructive, insidious ideas right inside the church! **He is trying to destroy the church from within**. This is indeed the *"Little Armageddon"*! How many are aware of this Little Armageddon? And, how many are prepared for the battle? Should we be prepared? Should especially leaders in the church be prepared?

Wait, just in case some reader might at this point be thinking, surely this is just an alarmist's work; it can't be that bad; it can't be that important; surely, we can just ignore the situation, it is not sufficiently important for us to pay it much attention; I advise that you stop here and read Chapter 32 of The Great Controversy, by Ellen G. White, entitled "Snares of Satan".

Also, here's a quote from Ellen White you may want to consider:

"We have ***far more to fear from within than from without***. The hindrances to strength and success are far greater from the church itself than from the world. Unbelievers have a right to expect that those who profess to be keeping the commandments of God and the faith of Jesus will do more than any other class to promote and honor, by their consistent lives, by their godly example and their active influence, the cause which they represent. But how often have the professed advocates of the truth proved the greatest obstacle to its advancement! The unbelief indulged, the doubts expressed, the darkness cherished, encourage the presence of evil angels, and open the way for the accomplishment of Satan's devices." {1SM 122.3: 1SM (1958) Chapter 16: Calls for Revival} Also in LDE 156.2 (1992) Chapter 11: Satan's Last Day Deceptions and RH, March 22, 1887 par. 4: The Church's Great Need.

This quote and the referenced chapter is applicable in more ways than one to the work being perpetrated by Satan and his demons and manifested through their agents, the Shepherd's Rods, in God's Remnant Church. One of Satan's devices to prevent a true revival in God's remnant church, which would result in the outpouring of the Holy Spirit and the finishing of the work of spreading the gospel, is to lead people into following falsehoods! That, dear friend, is a most effective weapon (poison) that destroys the desire for revival and witnessing. Many members are leaving the church through the "back door"; unfortunately, some are also being overtaken by offshoots and are leaving the church – right under our noses! It's full time that we get rid of some wolves – and save some sheep!

If I should extrapolate my personal experience to the general church population, I think it is quite possible that much of the younger generation of Seventh-day Adventists do not have a clue as to who these people, the Shepherd's Rods are, and how dangerous and divisive their activities. It is quite possible that there are many Seventh-day Adventists, young and, not so young; who were even "born in the message" and / or, are even second and third generation Seventh-day Adventists but have *never* even heard the name "Shepherd's Rod". I can just imagine someone saying: So what? What if I don't know? I don't have to know. However, not knowing the Shepherd's Rods and the nature of their work could prove to be rather dangerous. It would be okay if we could just stop there. However, the fact is that, in recent times, this offshoot group, seem to be increasing in numbers and have apparently stepped up their activities within the Seventh-day Adventist Church. Because of the nature of their work – as you shall see – the increase of their numbers is directly related to the decrease in our numbers. At the very least, recent happenings suggest that the group is pretty much alive and well – and determined to continue to recruit their members from among our ranks! There is much more that I could say in response to the questions posed but I will rest that issue with the following words from Hosea 4:6 "My people are destroyed for lack of knowledge:" (1st part)

The group is believed to have claimed many Seventh-day Adventist Christians over the years, with Leaders, Elders and even Pastors of the church to boot! Unfortunately, some of those Leaders, Elders, Pastors, felt themselves well, and strong, and capable of "dealing with them" (1 Cor. 10:12). The end results of some of those encounters are, in a word, sad. They thought they could stand, they thought they, in their own strength, were equal to the task – but, instead of convincing them to "come back to the fold", they themselves have joined their ranks.

Dear reader, God has all the answers for us and only total dependence on Him can keep us (1 Cor. 10:13, Phil. 4:13). The key is to make Jesus our **Lord** and **Savior**, study the Word diligently, get close to God and **be led by His Spirit in all that we do.** Dear reader, pray for the Holy Spirit to give you the gift of discernment and while you are at it pray for courage – because in this *Little Armageddon*, you will need that too! You just might find yourself standing alone! But take courage, if we are fully aware in this Great Controversy we know that technically, when you are standing for God you are **never** "alone" – because you and God are a majority! Moreover, one can take comfort in what one Seventh-day Adventist missionary sister said when she was faced with a very difficult and dangerous situation; she said: "I am **not** going in alone. There are at least five of us! There is **the Father, the Son, the Holy Spirit**, my **guardian angel** and **me!**" Praise the Lord!

By virtue of the fact that the Shepherd's Rods have been active in the Church for many years and that they seem to be increasing their efforts at dividing the Church and ***drawing away men after themselves***, we can indeed say that there is a Little Armageddon going on. Just as sure as there was war in Heaven there is war in the True Church today because the devil would like to destroy God's Church – any way he can. But he shall not prevail. Jesus and His Saints **will** triumph at last! (Rev. 14:12, Rev. 12:11, Matt. 28:18, Rev. 7:3, 4, 9, 10, 13 – 15) Praise the Lord!

The existence of offshoots, including the Shepherd's Rods (OR Davidians) have plagued the Seventh-day Adventist Church since the time when the Prophetess of the Remnant Church was alive. Two notable such persons that joined with those who believed and taught falsehoods were John Harvey Kellogg and Stephen Smith. Kellogg advocated Pantheism, which included the belief that God is just a mysterious essence or impersonal influence - God is in everything in nature; God is impersonal; as impersonal as sunshine. This was accepted and taught by many as new advanced truth. In reality it threatened the very foundations of the Biblical view of God. It threatened to destroy the Remnant Church. However, God, through His prophet Ellen G. White, settled the controversy.

Smith believed that he and those who believed like him had "new light". He began to spread his views that were not in harmony with the views held by the Church. He became bitter and critical of the Church leadership – especially James and Ellen White. Smith was dis-fellowshipped from the church. For many years he shifted his allegiance from one offshoot group after another. However, God used Ellen G. White and others to reach Smith and he was convicted as to the error of his beliefs and he eventually came back to the Remnant Church, abandoning his false beliefs. Praise the Lord! It is my hope that the members of the Shepherd's Rod groups that still exist so return to the fold from which they have gone astray.

This handbook, which I hope can fit snugly in your shirt or coat pocket, will be restricted to the Shepherd's Rods. The Shepherd's Rod offshoot groups believe that they have been appointed to "clean up" the Seventh-day Adventist Church and prepare a remnant out of the Remnant. This, they believe has become necessary because the Church is corrupt and has a lot of problems, with many sins practiced openly and widely in the Church. They believe, among other things, that the church leadership and church organization on a whole is not leading the church in the right path and that the tithes and offerings are being misused.

In summary, they believe that the Church is not perfect. I agree! Indeed the Seventh-day Adventist Church is not perfect! However, if it was, it could not be God's Church, because Jesus said ***the wheat and the tares*** must grow together ***until the day of harvest***! God knows that the Church is not perfect. In the book of Revelation (Chapters 2, 3) He says: "I know thy works" to each of the seven churches. However, His plan to clean up the Church ***does not involve the use of the Shepherd's Rods (or any other such group)***. God's plan to clean up the last day Church is through the fiery trials and persecutions to come late in the time of the end – just before the end of time. In other words, God's plan to clean up the Church has much to do with Armageddon! The Shaking, the Sifting and the Latter Rain[1] will purify and prepare the Church for its last work and successful stand against the beast and its image and, for overcoming in the battle of Armageddon (Revelation chapters 13, 14, 18, and so on).

So, if we can't overcome in the Little Armageddon what will happen to us then? Now is the time to prepare. "Be sober, be vigilant; because your adversary the devil, as a roaring lion walketh about seeking whom he may devour." (1 Peter 5:8).

This handbook you are reading was compiled because there seem to be a need to educate the general membership of the Seventh-day Adventist Church about this group but, also to help Leaders and Elders in the local churches to be "armed for warfare" by being forewarned and knowledgeable about

1 James 5:7, 8, COL Chaps. 2, 9, AA Chap. 5, CET 18: "Preparation for the end", 30: "The Shaking", 16: "To the little flock"; GC Chap. 39: "The time of trouble"; LS80 Chapter 19: "God's providences", etc.

the Shepherd's Rods and about the prophetic gift. As faithful Under-shepherds the leaders of the Seventh-day Adventist Church must be concerned and must become aware of the activities of these persons … and get involved in the war against this insidious group. If you are a member of God's True Remnant Church you are a target of Satan; a target of this group.

As you read this handbook I believe you will conclude that the Shepherd's Rod offshoot must have originated in the very mind of Satan and is a part of his arsenal to attack God's True Church in these days, the very last days of earth's history. I trust that you will find real practical information in its pages. The material presented is not intended to be either exhaustive or conclusive. Neither is it a philosophical presentation nor purports to be the total answer to the problem. Rather, the intention is to provide real ***practical*** information based on ***experience*** and to stimulate study and evoke an ***appropriate*** *response to this offshoot group.* The book seeks to offer the reader use-able, work-able strategies to deal with the Shepherd's Rod offshoot and also arm Church members with an ***easy reference tool*** – an easy to use weapon in the Little Armageddon that can be used to quickly find advice and to refresh one's memory on various aspects of the issue. It is hoped that this book will be the first in a series of manuals that will cover offshoot groups within the Seventh-day Adventist Church.

It is intended that *each chapter*, per se, will serve as an effective weapon in the warfare against satan and his demons and human agents manifested in the person and work of the Shepherd's Rods. The chapters give different perspectives and approaches to prepare for, get involved in and / or ***deal with*** the problem. It is hoped that each chapter will speak to the needs of the different readers in a unique way and provide some assistance in the battle in some way for each reader. Everyone is involved: If you are not a member of a Shepherd's Rod group it behooves you to educate yourself on the issue, guard your own soul and help to protect the other brethren. If you are a member of the group I believe that there is still hope for you; choose now to get back on the path of righteousness; come out of your apostatized state before it is too late!

Finally, it is hoped that this little handbook will serve to stimulate a greater zeal for the study of both the written and Living Word of God. I trust that that will be your experience.

*Dear reader, even with this handbook in your hand or coat pocket you will need much prayer for the guidance of the **Holy Spirit** to know how to deal with your particular situation in your particular church should you have to contend with these offshoots. For that matter, it is hoped that this handbook will inspire interest in both the Leaders and the general membership in the Seventh-day Adventist Church to really study the Word of God and <u>really get to know what the Church teaches / what Seventh-day Adventists really believe</u> (2 Tim. 2:15; please see "Seventh-day Adventists Believe", © 2005, Second Edition). This is absolutely crucial because **when you truly know the genuine (the truth in God's words) and <u>the One</u> who is <u>the way, the truth and the life</u>, the great "I Am" … you <u>cannot</u> be deceived by any counterfeit!***

Jumping to Conclusion

Jumping in into murky water is never good or safe. Especially, going headfirst is foolhardy; one needs to check out the waters – maybe put your feet first. In other words, make sure you know (for sure) what you are getting into. Of necessity, questions need to be asked. What kind of water is this? Why is it so murky? Where did it come from? Why and how did it start getting murky in the first place? How can I know for sure that the answers I am getting are reliable?

Militarily, it is very important to reconnoiter to ensure that the way is clear / that the way is safe before advancing troops. It is necessary to establish what exists on the battlefield. Knowing the field of battle can determine who wins the battle. When the territory is familiar to you – you will have the advantage.

2 Timothy 2:15 / John 5:39 / Isaiah 8:20

Chapter One

Edification on the Shepherd's Rod: Their Story

Introduction and Background Reading:

Many things are being used by satan and his hosts to attack and destroy God's church. These include intellectual, cultural and racial differences. However, an even more deadly attack is the attack on the foundational doctrines of the Seventh-day Adventist Church. The attack is made ultimately more dangerous as it is being perpetrated through those who have a close association with the church as, in many cases; they had been members for many years. Indeed, many of them still claim to be members of the church and pose as such. Hence, the attack is even more dangerous because it is made from within the body of Christ. From within it can often go unsuspected and have the result of a terrible, insidious poison[2].

It is this attack, this ***Little Armageddon*** that this book seeks to address. We, as a church and, as individuals must guard and fight against satan's attacks and deceptions wherever and whenever they are discovered. Very sadly, satan's attacks

---

2 Read the chapter on "Satan's Deception" in the book The Great Controversy by Ellen G. White.

go undiscovered in many churches, in many Conferences of the Seventh-day Adventist Church. This happens because unfortunately, the members are not studying the Bible and the Spirit of Prophecy Writings as they should. Those that do study are not studying enough and there are many that are not studying at all. On the other hand many members of the church are totally unaware of the attack, totally devoid of the knowledge that satan is waging a little war, a ***Little Armageddon*** in the church. Even more serious is the fact that many church members are just plain ignorant of the existence of the organized group through which these agents operate: the Shepherd's Rod group. This makes the attack especially deadly. Many saints are being ensnared and churches corrupted as a result of the activities of satan's representatives who pose as brethren blessed with special superior knowledge and higher light.

This book intends to educate the general church membership about this group and its activities and intentions by pulling heavily from resources available to the church.[3] These resources, although available through various means are not being read or utilized by the general membership and, even many leaders. Putting essential information together in one place and of a volume that encourages its reading, written simply so that anyone can understand it and containing instructions and advice that are practical and easy to follow will definitely help to prepare regular members and lay leaders alike to successfully resist and repel the attack. There is a very popular saying that "what you don't know wont hurt you". Of course, we know that that is absolutely false! In the case of the attacks that we are addressing in this book what you don't know might kill you. One can be led down a path that result in spiritual bankruptcy and even death

---

3   Mainly the S.D.A. Church Manual and S.D.A. Encyclopedia.

The Little Armageddon

and ultimately, even eternal death. So, this is an absolutely serious issue!

While the church is under vicious attack generally[4] and, indirectly through the false doctrines being perpetrated by many outside the church – such as the secret rapture, an eternally burning hell, etc., – the attack of which we speak is from within the church! For that reason this attack is particularly dangerous and deadly. A poison that is separated from food is much less dangerous and deadly than one that is mingled with a delicious meal[5]. The poisoned meal is that much more deadly because of its potential to deceive or go undetected. Similarly, when some of the genuine doctrines of the church are accepted and taught along with false, faith-destroying, soul-destroying doctrines –as the Shepherd's Rod do – many unsuspecting members can be deceived and destroyed. While I do not believe that the Shepherd's Rod group pose a serious threat to the general church body or world church at this time, I believe we do need to prepare the lay leadership and every individual church member to successfully counteract the attack of satan through this group wherever and whenever it manifests itself. One soul deceived, one soul ensnared, one soul that is lost because of lack of information, because of being unprepared for the attack is ***one soul too many!***

We cannot afford to leave this problem not directly addressed in some way. While we are evangelizing and gaining new members, planting churches, etc. we need to strengthen the members that are already with us as well as educate those coming in so that they can be prepared for the attack. This attack, this war, the ***Little Armageddon*** is one of the means satan is using to decrease the membership and lead

---

4   See 1 Peter 5:8 and Revelation 12:17.
5   Read The Great Controversy, chapter 36.

many souls to destruction. This is one of the countervailing forces satan has set up in Seventh-day Adventist church. As we allow the Lord to use us and God brings them in, satan ensnares them – right under our noses! We cannot afford to not do anything specific about it. This book, I believe, represents one way of dealing with the problem. It is time for a book like this, because it is time for us to get rid of some wolves – so we can save some sheep! More importantly, it is time for all of God's people to start to really study God's words because it is really our only safeguard against satan and his attacks[6]!

In this chapter we will draw upon available resources as a background and introduction before we look at what one of the Shepherd's Rod groups have to say for themselves regarding their history.

According to the *SDA Bible Student's Sourcebook:*

"Offshoots from larger churches have been common, with the result of separate churches that, however, hold almost the same beliefs. Thus, there are thirteen churches in the Reformed or Presbyterian group, twenty-four in the Baptist group and twenty-three in the Methodist group. Racial factors, as well as the influences of sectionalism, particularly the differences between North and South, have added to the divisions."

"On the other hand, the Seventh-day Adventist Church – the Remnant Church, has remained united throughout the years of its existence. This does not mean that divisions do not exist in any way in the Church[7] but that the official body

---

6 See The Great Controversy, chapter 37.
7 Some would say the existence of the so-called "Black Conference" and "White Conference" / "Black Church" and "White Church" is one such division that is like a sore on the unity of the SDA Church.

of believers has remained united in the fundamental beliefs despite the church being one with a worldwide presence. It is this unity that is threatened by the Shepherd's Rod."

Also, from the ***SDA Encyclopedia:***

Apostate Movements

Since the beginning of the Seventh-day Adventist Church various offshoots from it have appeared. Dr. J. H. Kellogg and prominent ministers such as A. T. Jones, D. M. Canright, and A. F. Ballenger, who left the SDA Church, did not lead organized movements of their own, although they did disagree with, and even oppose, some of the denomination's teachings and policies. The following are offshoot organizations, listed here in the order of the dates of their rise:

- The *Messenger* Party and "Age to Come" Defection (1853–1855)
- The *Hope of Israel* and Marion Party (1858–1863)
- The SDA Reform Movement — German (1915)
- The Reformed SDAs — Rowenite (1916)
- The Shepherd's Rod movement, or Davidian SDAs (1929)
- The United Sabbath Day Adventists (1930).

Hence, we discover that the Shepherd's Rod group is an offshoot of the Seventh-day Adventist church. So, the members of that group are not members of the main church or body of believers. Now, since we are writing about the Shepherd's Rod group it would be good to hear from them. Let us look at what they say.

The First Salvo: What Does the Other Side Have to Say for Themselves?

A Brief History (by a Shepherd's Rod group)

The Shepherd's Rod movement as it is popularly known, was derived from a series of controversial Biblical Studies presented initially in Los Angeles, California, in the 1930's by Victor Tasho Houteff, A Bulgarian Émigré, and while a Sabbath School Teacher in a Los Angeles local Seventh-day Adventist church.

Victor Tasho Houteff was born in Raicovo, Bulgaria, March 2, 1885, and became a member of the Greek Orthodox Church before emigrating to the United States in 1907. In 1919, while running a small hotel in the mid-west, he joined the Seventh-day Adventist Denomination / Church. By 1923, Bro. Houteff relocated to Los Angeles, California, where he became a respected and popular church member and Sabbath School Teacher. His lessons revealed new and startling expositions of countless Biblical passages. While not contradicting the church's fundamental doctrines, he called for a world-wide denominational reform, and brought "new light" to SDA eschatology. Those new teachings subsequently brought a wave of persecution to believers who were convinced of its veracity and that it was divinely inspired truth. Its theological positions posed a gargantuan challenge to SDA clergy and laity. Its explications and exegeses were so compelling that even some high ranking officials embraced the message.

In 1930 Bro Houteff published his first Volume, entitled, "The Shepherd's Rod, Volume 1". He published a 2nd (Shepherd's Rod, Volume II) in 1932. This of course did not stop the persecution. In fact, it intensified. This brought on a series of confrontations involving believers being verbally

The Little Armageddon

and physically abused. Church leaders numerous times and with varying methods, attempted unsuccessfully to stamp out the fledgling movement.

Finding no other recourse, Rod believers organized the Universal Publishing Association in 1934, in Los Angeles, California. In 1935 he established a training center, and Headquarters in Waco, Texas, where for about 20 years the ministry catapulted the message to Adventists world-wide. It published and dispensed millions of pieces of literature, initiated and employed hundreds of workers, all the while building an expansive institution with 389 acres - with crop farming, houses, horses, goats, a dairy farm, orchards, and an apiary. It had its own water supply, dispensary, mercantile, chapel and Bible Training School. Up to 125 persons resided at the Center--mostly staff and their families. By the mid 1950's its regular subscribers numbered about 100,000 worldwide. The Denomination numbering just over 800,000. It was during this period that "Rod" believers became known as Davidian Seventh-day Adventists.

On February 5, 1955, Victor Houteff died at Hillcrest Hospital, Waco, Texas of heart failure. His wife was elected the Chairman of the Executive Council, but through a series of unfortunate and ill-advised decisions and predictions, plunged the movement into disrepute, especially when the new Council forecasted the establishment of the Kingdom in April 22, 1959. This debacle became known as the "knock-out blow" and subsequently caused the movement to fragment, and the Association dissolved.

Since that time, orthodox believers have reorganized endeavoring to carry the original, untainted, message to the SDA denomination in harmony with Bro. Houteff's original writings. Believers still number in the thousands, but continue to face stiff opposition from the Church's hierarchy--believers still battle unrelenting prejudice and persecution. Furthermore, they have to confront radical and fanatical elements who start their own groups and introduce strained and contradictory teachings, completely out of harmony with the Bible, the teachings of the church and Victor Houteff's message.

The General Association of Davidian Seventh-day Adventists remains true to the original teachings as expounded from the Scriptures and the writings of Mrs. E. G. White, the church's Inspired founder. It holds true as its original forbearers, that the Shepherd's Rod Message is God's voice--His revelation today to the SDA Church Denomination. We are convinced because of the overwhelming Biblical evidence. That is, despite the skeptics, its persecutors and fanatics, its teachings' rooted deep in the Holy Scriptures convince us that we have not followed "cunningly devised fables". (2 Pet. 1:16).

As we have seen the Shepherd's Rod group is only one of the offshoot groups. If this account is taken as typical and applicable to all the groups, this group is not one to be taken lightly or ignored. By their own testimony they are very stubborn and difficult to get rid of. Dear reader, Satan is determined to deceive, he knows the Bible well and you should expect that he will, through the groups he has set up, claim to be the one with the truth. This is typical Satan strategy. But Satan is still the father of lies, as he was from the beginning (John 8:44), and no liar is to be believed. So, what then? In our second chapter we will look at what the church says about the group.

Chapter Two

Edification on the Shepherd's Rod: The Church's Story

Return Salvo!
What Does the Remnant Church Have to Say?

Dear reader, what does the Seventh-day Adventist Church have to say about the Shepherd's Rod group? For an answer let's go to the Seventh-day Adventist Encyclopedia. What does it say on the Shepherd's Rod? Read on:

DAVIDIAN SEVENTH-DAY ADVENTISTS - SHEPHERD'S ROD.

An offshoot launched by Victor T. Houteff, a member of a Seventh-day Adventist church in Los Angeles, California, in 1929, popularly called the "Shepherd's Rod," after the title of his first publication. His organization took the name of "Davidian Seventh-day Adventists" in 1942. **Houteff, who regarded himself as a divinely inspired messenger of God** *(Author's emphasis)* set forth succinctly the primary subject of his teaching in his first publication as follows: "This publication contains only one main subject with a double lesson; namely, the 144,000 [of Rev. 7:4–9; 14:1] and a call for reformation" (The Shepherd's Rod, first ed. [1930], vol. 1, p. 11).

In May 1935 Houteff and 11 followers (including children) migrated from California to Waco, Texas, and established a colony on a nearby farm, which they referred to thereafter as **Mount Carmel Center**. This center was *intended to be the temporary headquarters for the assembling of the 144,000 sealed ones, preparatory to their transfer to Palestine as the re-established kingdom of David under a theocratic regime, there to direct the closing work of the gospel on earth prior to the second advent of Christ. (Author's emphasis)*.

Prior to his death on Feb. 5, 1955, Houteff had appointed his wife to lead his flock until the Lord should choose another prophet to take charge of it. The Waco Tribune-Herald of Feb. 27, 1955, reported shortly after Houteff's death that at one time there had been as many as 125 persons living at the Mount Carmel Center, including children and some invalids in the rest home.

Immediately after Houteff's death the Shepherd's Rod party began to break up into splinter groups. The main body, under Mrs. Houteff's leadership, **announced in print to the public that the prophetic period of 1260 days foretold in Rev. 11 would end on Apr. 22, 1959, and that on that date God would intervene in a remarkable manner in Palestine to clear out both the Jews and the Arabs for the establishment of the Davidic kingdom in that country.** Responding to an official call to assemble at their Waco headquarters during Apr. 16–22, 1959, in readiness to move to Palestine as soon as Providence should indicate, several hundred persons gathered at the Mount

Carmel Center to await the fulfillment of the prediction. *When the date passed uneventfully, most of the people-disappointed, confused, and embarrassed-scattered slowly from Waco to begin life anew elsewhere as best they could.* **Some returned to the SDA Church, some lost all faith in the Bible and strayed off into the world**[8], and some joined splinter groups, such as "the Branch" (which actually sent a few colonizers to Israel in a mission that has ended in failure). Some stayed with the Waco leaders to face the future.

Mrs. Houteff and her associate leaders frankly and publicly acknowledged in print on Dec. 12, 1961, and Jan. 16, 1962, that the Shepherd's Rod party and its peculiar teachings were not sound. Finally, on Mar. 11, 1962, they resigned, declared the Davidian Association dissolved, closed their Mount Carmel Center, and put the property up for sale. Having done this, they scattered. (Emphasis, sic)

Subsequent to Mrs. Houteff's disbanding of the organization, *several groups persisted, each claiming to be the authentic successor to the Shepherd's Rod party.*

One of these groups, calling themselves Branch Davidian Seventh-day Adventists, established a center, again near Waco, which in 1984 came under the control of Vernon Howell, who in 1981 had been dis-fellowshipped from the Tyler, Texas, Seventh-day Adventist Church. Later Howell changed his name to David Koresh, a name adopted from the Semitic form of the name of Cyrus, the Persian ruler of the sixth century B.C. In addition to pressing his claim to the prophetic gift, he presented himself as a latter-day

---

8   2. Ellen White re The Platform

fulfillment of the roles of David and Cyrus as deliverers of God's people.

Howell (Koresh) traveled widely, recruiting members for his community, especially in Australia and Great Britain. His special teachings, based on an interpretation of Ezekiel 9 and the seven seals of Revelation, led to a heightened sense of impending attack, for which in preparation a large quantity of firearms was stockpiled in the Davidian headquarters.

On Feb. 28, 1993, the Davidian community was surrounded by law-enforcement authorities, leading to extensive gunfire and the death of several persons, both within the building and of officers outside. A tense state of siege continued, until on Apr. 19, 1993, during an attack by officers, fire broke out in the building, destroying the wooden structure and killing approximately 90 persons inside.

Since destruction of the Branch Davidian community, several other splinter groups remain as remnants of the Shepherd's Rod movement. *(End of article)*

From the above we gather that the Shepherd's Rod group is really not one group but many groups – a *splintered* foe. They have one thing in common – they embrace and teach falsehood. Today they exist in many Conferences of the church. We have a battle on our hands! The group(s) is not localized to a particular area but are scattered abroad, infiltrating many churches – perhaps worldwide? Huh? In our next chapter we will look at the group more closely. Please note that the other name for the group we will consider is *Davidian Seventh-day Adventist*.

Equality is claimed.

Anyone can claim to be something. But how do you know a pudding is really a pudding? If you had the experience of actually eating a genuine pudding before would that help you to determine if this thing in front of you is indeed a pudding?

Militarily, it is good to be able to establish ***true identity*** – camouflage and stealth can lead to success where otherwise it would be impossible. Being aware of what is what and who is who / knowing your environment is absolutely crucial to success in the Christian warfare. We must know the enemy / be able to identify the enemy – no matter what disguise they use. This is very important.

Ephesians 4:5

Chapter Three

Cooperation and Unity Will Help Us to Overcome in the Battle of the Little Armageddon!

Some Heat in the Little Armageddon: A Battle Royal!

Dear Reader, scenes of much physical and spiritual conflict and confrontations between Shepherd's Rods and vigilant Leaders in the Local Seventh-day Adventist Church at which I was baptized are firmly embedded in my mind. I have seen Shepherd's Rods boldly and fearlessly challenge Church Elders openly and have offered physical resistance when asked to leave the Church. I know of a Church literally **invaded** by a host of Shepherd's Rods … they came to take over the church! But the Elders and the Deacons and some other members would not have it so! It was a battle royal! I have seen the conflict gotten so bad that real physical fights would have resulted (there was some pushing and shoving) … and the police had to be called to get them out of the Church!

The Little Armageddon

The attacks in that Church came in waves … and sometimes these waves were tidal waves; real massive onslaughts! Some of what I know of such confrontations in that Local Church was told to me by other members that were there before me.

There was at least one Shepherd's Rod that was usually around … even in the quiet times. I am happy that God had an extremely vigilant Holy Spirit led First Elder at that Church. He was very diligent, very protective of us members…and he taught and trained his flock very well as a good Under-shepherd should[9]. God blessed him! And keeps on blessing him even today. Maybe if it were not for that determined, Spirit-filled Elder many persons (especially young converts … as I was) would be deceived and might have left the Church. Furthermore, many of us were torn by the conflicts but we did not leave the ship of Zion. We held on to what we knew as truth! Because we were constantly fed the truth through Bible Classes (two per week) and Pointed Doctrinal Preaching and we were shown love by the Leaders of the church.

I had the experience of knowing Shepherd's Rods personally. I have had my run of disputes with Shepherd's Rods and, I can tell you - they are very stubborn … and so steeped in their deception, even when the plain "thus saith the Lord" faces them, they still hold on to their falsehood. I am now a not so young Seventh-day Adventist Christian having been in the Church for over thirty years. I am now myself very privileged to be a Local Elder in the Remnant Church of God … God forbid that I should allow such false teachers to wreak havoc in God's Church! If and when they come … how could I ever just stand by and do *nothing*? **God forbid**!

---

9   Jesus told Peter: "Feed my sheep." (John 21:16, 17)

> *Dear Readers. Seventh-day Adventist Christians: Let us pray to God and study our Bibles every day ... and get to know Jesus Christ as our Personal Savior and Lord. This is imperative. We are indeed living in the time of the end ... the activity of the Shepherd's Rods is but one of the signs ... one small inkling of the Armageddon to come ... and already the devil has marshaled a mighty force ... I believe he is getting ready to launch a major attack soon. Soldiers of Christ, arise! Put your armor on! (Eph.6: 10-18)*

Marshalling a valuable weapon through cooperation:

The following article taken from the Beacon Light Tapes Ministry's website on TAGnet[10] should help greatly in repelling Satan's attacks. I found it to be very informative, instructive and inspiring. I couldn't do any better in writing a similar article myself ... the depth of research that is evidenced I would be unable to accomplish in a short time ... and it was impressed on me that information such as contained in this article is needed and must be made available as part of a work such as this. The Holy Spirit literally led me to this article as I was on the Internet one day. After contacting the Beacon Light Tapes Ministry I corresponded with the author of the article and he graciously agreed that the article could be a part of the book I was preparing on the Shepherd's Rod group. He gave me much encouragement. As far as he was concerned he was happy and privileged to be a part of the efforts being made to nullify the effects of the activities of the Shepherd's Rod groups.

One of the strengths of the article is that it gives a pretty good comparative analysis of Ellen White and Victor Houteff's

---

10 Now, Advent Source.

messages in some key areas.[11] Emphases throughout the article are those of its writer as the article is presented in its original state.

We already pointed out in the previous chapter that another name for the group is the Davidian Seventh-day Adventists. Hence, the title of the article:

Dear reader, pray earnestly … then *read well*:

Article Begins Here

WHO ARE THE DAVIDIAN SEVENTH-DAY ADVENTISTS?

Introduction

From time to time, members of the Seventh-day Adventist Church come in contact with or hear about individuals who call themselves Davidian Seventh-day Adventists. There are actually several different groups that call themselves Davidians, and each group has their own unique version of "truth." Until the Branch Davidians received so much notoriety in Waco, Texas a few years ago, many Seventh-day Adventists had never heard of Davidians. David Koresh and 78 Davidians died in a fire at Mount Carmel on April 19, 1993, ending a 51-day standoff with federal authorities. Many Davidian groups are quick to demonize Koresh and point out that their particular group is in no way connected to Koresh's group.

Several Davidian groups maintain web sites on the Internet. Some of them pose as genuine Seventh-day Adventists in order to lure unsuspecting Adventists into reading their material or joining their discussion groups. Examples of

---

11 It was written by Dwight Turner and is used here in its entirety by his kind, enthusiastic permission.

Davidian web site names are: "Bread of Life," "Arms of God," "Quiet Moments," "SDA Pioneers" (this one truly appears to be a genuine Seventh-day Adventist site but is in reality a front for Davidians), and "Shepherd's Rod Information Center." At these web sites one will find quotes by Ellen White, references to the 27 Fundamental Beliefs of Seventh-day Adventists, health topics, and other indicators that would lead unsuspecting readers to conclude that the goal of the web site is to edify and educate church members on the Spirit of Prophecy and other topics of interest to Seventh-day Adventists. One must sometimes explore quite far into the web site before being able to determine that the ultimate goal of the site is to propagate Davidian heresies.

The term *Shepherd's Rod* is often associated with Davidians because they all claim belief in the writings of the late Victor Houteff. Over several years Houteff authored a series of publications which are now referred to as the *Shepherd's Rod*. Although Houteff's writings provide the basis for the beliefs of all the different Davidian groups, it is important to note that *each group has their own particular interpretation of those writings*. The fact that their teachings differ so much from each other makes it difficult to discuss their beliefs, for no matter what subject one attempts to deal with, a spokesman from at least one Davidian group will protest that "we don't believe that!" or "you have misrepresented the message!"

Notwithstanding the fact that each Davidian group has their own unique set of doctrines, it is still worthwhile to seek to discover more about Davidians and how their beliefs differ from that of traditional Seventh-day Adventists. Davidians have never posed a major threat to the Seventh-day Adventist organization; but each year they have been able to lure a few unsuspecting (and usually disgruntled) church members into their fold.

The Little Armageddon

The General Conference of Seventh-day Adventists has provided much written material over the past sixty years designed to educate their members about the Davidian SDA groups, but many of our members do not know this material is available or how to obtain copies of it. The information contained in this article draws heavily from that published material as well as from many personal observations of the author.

What Do They Believe?

Davidians believe that the writings of the late Victor T. Houteff contain "new light" for the Seventh-day Adventist Church. In an official publication, one Davidian group claims that they hold several fundamental doctrines in common with the Seventh-day Adventist Church. Twenty-two doctrines are listed which are taken from the *Year Book of the Seventh-day Adventist Denomination*, 1940 edition, which defines such doctrines as the Trinity, the divinity of Christ, the unchangeable law of ten commandments, the final destruction of the wicked, etc.

Following the list of common doctrines, it is then stated that "In addition to these fundamental tenets of faith held in common with the Seventh-day Adventists, the Davidian Association holds…,"—and then fifteen additional beliefs are listed, few of which have anything at all in common with established Seventh-day Adventist beliefs. (See *Fundamental Beliefs and Directory of the Davidian Seventh-day Adventists*, 1943, pp 11-15.)

Again taking into account that each group has their own unique twist on doctrine, Davidians in general believe that, prior to the Loud Cry, a call will go out for all *Shepherd's Rod* followers to travel to old Jerusalem where David's throne will be set up upon which a "man" who is not Christ will sit to "judge" and "seek judgment." From Jerusalem, that group (the 144,000) will go out to proclaim the Loud Cry, the results of which will be the conversion of the "great multitude" of Revelation 7:9. Davidians believe they have been called out of the "decadent" Seventh-day Adventist Church, and thus have become the remnant of the remnant. They also claim that all Seventh-day Adventists who do not accept their doctrines will be slaughtered *prior* to the Loud Cry by angels wielding swords. They teach that there will be *two* more advents of Christ, an *invisible* one at which the kingdom will be established in old Jerusalem, and later a *visible* return after the Loud Cry is complete when both the 144,000 and the "great multitude" will be translated to heaven.

Seventh-day Adventists who are familiar with the sequence of major events that will take place from the present time to the return of Jesus can readily see from the above brief outline that the views of Davidian SDAs are definitely not in accordance with established church doctrine. Church officials, after years of examining Davidian beliefs, concluded and officially declared that the *Shepherd's Rod* contains heresy. And yet Davidians are put off and offended by the fact that they are referred to as offshoots and heretics, and are not allowed membership in the organized Seventh-day Adventist Church.

Mrs. White wrote that **"A line of truth extending from that time** [when our church pioneers hammered out our distinct doctrines] **to the time when we shall enter the city of God, was made plain to me."** Series B, No. 2, p 57. Our Davidian friends would have us believe that the time line the Lord "made plain" to Ellen White did not include such important events as the setting up of a temporal kingdom in Jerusalem and the slaughter of Seventh-day Adventists who refuse to change their allegiance from the Seventh-day Adventist Church to the Davidian SDA Association.

One may argue that there may well be other events that will happen that were not distinctly revealed to Mrs. White. However, we must assert that if any claim of new events not revealed to Mrs. White is found to be out of harmony with the events that God *did* reveal to her is to be rejected as error. Seventh-day Adventist scholars and theologians, after many years of examining the events that the teachings of the *Shepherd's Rod* claim will happen before we enter the city of God, have conclusively determined that those events are indeed totally out of harmony with light that was revealed to Mrs. White.

V. T. Houteff's Hidden Agenda

Seventh-day Adventists are puzzled as to why people with such differing views from their own insist that they are genuine Seventh-day Adventists. The real reason that Victor Houteff, founder of the Shepherd's Rod movement, wanted his followers to remain associated with the Seventh-day Adventist Church is brought to light in the following statement taken from an article compiled by The Committee on Defense Literature of the General Conference of Seventh-day Adventists: "It was Mr. Houteff's hope in the beginning that he might remain in the Seventh-day Adventist Church and leaven its membership with his peculiar teachings, and reform and reorganize the denominational organization in conformity with his wishes. He did not at first want to start a new church, or denomination, of his own, although he and his handful of followers had organized themselves outside of the Seventh-day Adventist Church on March 12, 1934. In order to achieve his objective he tried to keep as many of his followers and sympathizers as possible in the Seventh-day Adventist Church, in order that they might bore from within. At the same time he wanted as much of the tithes and offerings as possible to flow out to him, in order that he and his organization might bore from without. On January 15, 1935, he bitterly denounced, as both wicked and foolish, the policies of the Seventh-day Adventist Church regarding the use of the tithes and offerings, since they barred such men as himself and his agents from making use of them for the furtherance of his work. One month later, —on February 15—he urged all of his sympathizers who could do so to remain in Seventh-day Adventist churches, saying: 'Hence, if we separate ourselves by staying away from the churches, we give them the opportunity to accuse us of being an offshoot from the body, and ourselves lose the occasion to contact the people. Moreover, if we separate ourselves from the organization, then in the fulfillment of Ezekiel 9, when those who have not the mark are taken away [Seventh-day Adventists slaughtered by angels], we shall have no right to claim possession of the denomination.'" *The History and Teachings of "The Shepherd's Rod"*, October 1955.

Thus it is clear that Houteff's goal from the beginning was "*to claim possession of the denomination.*" Neither Houteff during his lifetime nor any of the scattered remnants of his original organization have ever come close to achieving that goal.

The History of the Shepherd's Rod Movement

Victor T. Houteff was born in Raikovo, Bulgaria, March 2, 1885, and died at Waco, Texas on February 5, 1955. Because of controversies with the leaders of the Greek Orthodox Church and with the Bulgarian government, Houteff was expelled from the country of his birth. In 1907, he migrated

The Little Armageddon

to the United States where he was baptized into the Seventh-day Adventist Church in the year 1919.

Houteff had a sour experience at one of the denomination's sanitariums which resulted in his critical attack on our institutions, claiming the people running them "are reactionaries, they are the modern priests, scribes and Pharisees…." V. T. Houteff, *Timely Greetings*, vol. 2, no. 35, (address of April 24, 1948), pp 12-16.

In 1929, while serving as an assistant superintendent of the Sabbath School at his home church in the Olympic Exposition Park area of Los Angeles, Houteff began to bring in his own peculiar ideas. He began to share his new beliefs with a few fellow members; but soon complaints were being lodged against him that what he was teaching was not in accordance with Seventh-day Adventists beliefs. After persistently refusing to cease teaching that which church leaders considered to be error, he was finally disfellowshipped.

Houteff often made the claim that the leadership in the Seventh-day Adventist Church never gave him a fair hearing; but it is the consensus of church leaders that he was afforded every opportunity to present his ideas to some of the leading brethren and argue his position from the Bible and writings of Ellen White. It was not until he refused to stop teaching his particular views to other Adventists that Houteff was finally dropped from membership.

In opposition to all the counsel given him, he released his teachings in printed form, issuing a book titled *The Shepherd's Rod* in December of 1930. He mailed copies to many denominational workers trying to gain their support. Continued efforts were made to save the man from heresy, but in spite of the conclusion of the leading church brethren that his views contained error, Houteff continued to build upon his theories by publishing a series of tracts in 1933.

Many hearings were provided to allow Houteff to present his ideas and have them be put to the test of Scripture; but as is so often the case when an individual arises claiming to have new light for the church, he persisted in his belief that he was right and that all those church leaders in California who had examined his writings were wrong.

Copies of his writings reached the denominational leaders in Washington, DC, and the brethren there also quickly determined that Houteff's teachings contained error. After discussing the matter, the General Conference Committee voted to prepare a leaflet to counteract the false teachings of *The Shepherd's Rod*.

While his teachings were being examined by different groups of church brethren, Houteff signed with his own hand a letter which contained two solemn promises. The first was this: "In case the committee find error in the teaching of 'The Shepherd's Rod,' and are able to refute same by the teachings of the Bible and the Spirit of Prophecy, Brother Houteff agrees to renounce the advocacy of the 'Shepherd's Rod,' and to make public renunciation of same." The second promise signed by Houteff was that "Brother Houteff also agrees to discontinue the propagation of the 'Shepherd's Rod,' so far as he can control same, in the Pacific Union Conference, during the time this investigation is being made." *The History and Teachings of The Shepherd's Rod*, October 1955, p 15.

Yet during the time the investigation was being made, Houteff proceeded to organize his few followers into an association, with himself as its leader. In spite of the fact that the committees that investigated his writings found much error, he never renounced his writings as he had promised.

In 1934, the Autumn Council, with representatives from the various divisions of the worldwide Seventh-day Adventist organization present, declared formally that: "Whereas, it is of paramount importance that Seventh-day Adventists should be united in teaching the distinctive truths of our message, and in meeting subversive errors; therefore, *Resolved*, That we, the delegates to the 1934 Biennial Council, hereby approve the principles contained in the current booklet, 'A Warning Against Error,' as prepared by the General Conference Committee, and that we likewise endorse the similar booklet published by the Pacific Press." Thus, the church formally declared that Houteff's teachings contained "subversive error."

In 1935, Houteff purchased 189 acres near Waco, Texas and established a colony called Mt. Carmel Center. In August of that same year, he pronounced: "True we are establishing our headquarters on this mount that is found in prophecy, but our stay here shall be very, very short." *The Symbolic Code*, vol. 1, no. 14 (August 1935), p 5. Houteff believed that soon he and his followers would relocate to the Holy Land and there set up the temporal kingdom of David. Twenty years later, according to the Waco *Tribune-Herald*, the colony had about 90 people living at the center. And as we are all painfully aware, almost 60 years after the establishment of the place where the Houteff's followers were to be only a "very, very short" time, the compound was burned to the ground.

In 1937, the group at Mt. Carmel was reorganized under the name of "The General Association of the Shepherd's Rod

Seventh-day Adventists." There was at that time a controversy within the organization over the fact that officers were not elected, but were appointed by Houteff himself.

During World War II, the group again reorganized under the name of "The Davidian Seventh-day Adventists," and set about to constitute themselves with formal membership and to bestow ministerial credentials so that their male members would be able to avoid being drafted into the military service.

No longer could they hide behind the claim that they were bona fide members and representatives of the Seventh-day Adventist Church. By their organizing and issuing certificates of membership to their followers, they confirmed the proclamation that had all along been made by genuine Seventh-day Adventists—that the Shepherd's Rod was nothing more or less than an offshoot of the church. Over the years, the following inspired statement from the pen of Ellen White has proven to be an insurmountable barrier against successful Davidian infiltration into the Seventh-day Adventist Church: **"God has a church upon the earth, who are His chosen people….He is leading, not stray offshoots, not one here and one there, but a people."** *Testimonies to Ministers*, p 61.

In 1935, Houteff tried to evade the term "offshoot" by instructing his followers to remain within the ranks of the Seventh-day Adventist Church. But later when they drew up their constitution, bylaws, and a general statement of their beliefs and practices as a church body in a document they titled *The Leviticus of the Davidian Seventh-day Adventists*, Houteff realized that it would be useless to keep on trying to hide the fact that his group was an offshoot; so he decided to acknowledge that fact by announcing that "The Davidians

The Little Armageddon

are an upshoot from decadent Seventh-day Adventism." *The Leviticus of the Davidian Seventh-day Adventists*, p 12.

In order to justify their existence as a separate church body, Davidian SDAs level charges of corruption and decadence against the remnant church, and in so doing they have entered into a work that would tear down the organized work that the Lord set up in the year 1863 known as the Seventh-day Adventist Church. **"Those who start up to proclaim a message on their own individual responsibility, who, while claiming to be taught and led of God, still make it their special work to tear down that which God has been for years building up, are not doing the will of God. Be it known that these men are on the side of the great deceiver. Believe them not....They will deride the order of the ministry as a system of priestcraft. From such turn away, have no fellowship with their message, however much they may quote the *Testimonies* and seek to entrench themselves behind them. Receive them not, for God has not given them this work to do."** *Testimonies to Ministers*, p 51.

After Houteff died in 1955, his widow along with the help of a few other leaders led his flock. On November 9 of that same year, "light" was received by the leaders at the Mt. Carmel center in Texas concerning events that were soon to transpire. A call went out that all believers in the *Shepherd's Rod* were to assemble at Mt. Carmel by April 16, 1959. A press announcement was generated from Mt. Carmel which stated: "We expect that sometime this spring God will commence to set up His peaceful kingdom in the Holy Land. We believe that the Holy Land will be prepared for the setting up of God's kingdom by the war of Zechariah 14....The April 22 date was calculated from the symbolic prophecy of the 1260 literal days of Revelation

11:3-6. Those days commenced November 9, 1955, and will end April 22, 1959. The events of verses 7 to 13 [that God will set up a king over all the earth, Jerusalem will be "safely inhabited," the Jews will be driven from Palestine, and a plague will fall upon all who have fought against Jerusalem] are to be fulfilled after April 22." *Review & Herald*, May 17, 1962, article titled "The Shepherd's Rod Organization Disbands."

Also as part of their predictions, the Davidian SDA leaders affirmed that "We believe also that sometime this spring God will in a direct and terrible judgment as shown in Isaiah 66:15-20 and Ezekiel the ninth chapter, remove all the hypocrites from the Seventh-day Adventist denomination and also from among the Davidians." This was to be the long-threatened slaughter of Seventh-day Adventists who refused to accept Houteff's doctrines.

Close to one thousand people loyal to the *Shepherd's Rod*, including some who belonged to splinter groups, left all their possessions behind and gathered at Mt. Carmel. But after weeks, and finally months, passed without the predicted events taking place, the disillusioned souls, many of them who were now penniless, left Mt. Carmel in confused disarray to begin their lives again elsewhere. Some repented of their folly and returned to once again become loyal members of the Seventh-day Adventist Church.

Had those deluded souls been ardent students of the Spirit of Prophecy as they claimed to be, they would not have fallen for any "time prophecy," for Mrs. White made it clear that after 1844, there would be no more time prophecies. That is, there were no more dates that could be calculated from Scripture upon which were to occur prophesied events. Mrs. White put it this way: **"Time has not been a test**

since 1844, and it will never again be a test. The Lord has shown me that the message of the third angel must go, and be proclaimed to the scattered children of the Lord, but it must not be hung on time. I say that some were getting a false excitement, arising from preaching time...." *The Seventh-day Adventist Bible Commentary*, vol 7, p 971. Also: **"Let all our brethren and sisters beware of anyone who would set a time for the Lord to fulfill His word in regard to His coming, or in regard to any other promise He has made of significance."** *Early Writings*, p 75.

Shortly after that embarrassing experience which received worldwide attention, the Mount Carmel leaders requested and were given a hearing at the Seventh-day Adventist World Headquarters in Takoma Park, Maryland. During several meetings lasting a total of about 50 hours, the Davidian SDA leaders presented their foremost peculiar doctrines to the leaders of the Seventh-day Adventist denomination; but when discussing the prophecies of Revelation, it was conceded by the Davidian spokesmen that their interpretation of these texts were out of harmony with Mrs. White's interpretation.

Seventh-day Adventist leaders took the opportunity to point out the several other inconsistencies between the teachings of the *Shepherd's Rod* and the Spirit of Prophecy. Before the meetings concluded, the Davidian SDA representatives, because they could not meet the arguments presented to them from the Spirit of Prophecy, submitted a written motion requesting the elimination of Mrs. White's writings in the further study of Bible prophecies—and this in the face of Houteff's assertion that "The interpretation of these scriptures [dealing with prophecies in Revelation] is supported entirely by the writings of Sr. E. G. White, that is termed the Spirit of Prophecy." *The Shepherd's Rod*, Vol. 1 (1930), p 11.

Earnest appeals by General Conference brethren were made to the Davidian SDA leaders, urging them to acknowledge their mistakes and unite with the Seventh-day Adventist Church to finish the work. [Note: a full copy of the "Report of a Meeting Between a Group of 'Shepherd's Rod' Leaders and a Group of General Conference Ministers, July 27 – August 7, 1959" is available from the General Conference of Seventh-day Adventists located in Silver Spring, Maryland.]

After the Davidian SDA representatives returned to Waco, Texas, bickering broke out amongst the leaders. Some who had attended the meetings at the General Conference were honest enough to admit the inconsistencies between Mrs. White's writings and those of V. T. Houteff, and left the group. A few splinter groups formed and broke away. Censure was heaped upon the leaders for the time-setting fiasco of April 22, 1959.

Then, in a newsletter from Mt. Carmel dated December 12, 1961, came the announcement that their beloved founder's teaching concerning Ezekiel 4 and 9 was at variance with the Bible. To the dismay of the few *Shepherd's Rod* believers who remained at that point, the Mt. Carmel leaders wrote: "Inasmuch, however, as the 'Rod' literature contains this misunderstanding on Ezekiel 9 and Ezekiel 4, (there are still other things which we have not dealt with as yet), its [Houteff's interpretation of those Bible texts] further use is impossible. If the literature [Houteff's writings] can no longer be used, it naturally follows that the work it promotes [there in Mt. Carmel] is automatically stopped....Now that we have discovered that the 'Rod' is not in harmony with the Bible on basic subjects, we understand why the 1959 [time setting] test turned out as it did." *The Symbolic Code*, February, 1962, pp 6, 7.

In March of 1962, the leaders at Mt. Carmel formally submitted their "Notice of Resignation" in which they wrote: "But in our thorough examination of the 'Rod' in the light of the Bible, we came upon the realization that adjustments in many of our doctrines were required if there was to be harmony between them and the Bible. For we discovered that some cardinal teachings were predicated on concepts Brother Houteff and I or Sister White expounded which the Bible actually does not support....There is no alternative open to us but to resign since, as we view it, so vital a change in the basic doctrines is involved that it leaves the [Davidian] Association without its declared prophetic commission." On March 11, 1962, it was formally resolved that "said General Association of Davidian Seventh-day Adventists be, and the same hereby is, dissolved, and shall henceforth cease to exist." *Review & Herald*, May 17, 1962, article titled "The Shepherd's Rod Organization Disbands." The Mt. Carmel center was officially closed, its leaders left, and the property and assets of the organization were left in the hands of an attorney.

In a letter dated October 16, 1989, and written to the pastor of a Seventh-day Adventist church in Vermont, Frank Holbrook, at that time the Associate Director of the Biblical Research Institute at the General Conference of Seventh-day Adventists, wrote: "But in the early '60s she [Mrs. Houteff] and her officers resigned and gave up the beliefs. This was sufficient—we thought—to destroy the "movement," and for about 20-25 years it was for all practical purposes dead. However, in recent years at least a dozen splinter groups have come into existence. They are separate and independent of each other—nor do they pull together.

"One of these groups—in the Waco area—is teaching that the Holy Spirit is of female gender! That group is so bizarre that it does not affect our people to any degree. But the group in Exeter, Missouri, is quite active and claims to be the one and only true descendant of the original Rod group....

"While there may be some new wrinkles (one group in Canada claims a prophet in their midst; and some of them are teaching that it is a sin to use credit cards), as far as we can tell, their basic doctrinal positions (based on misinterpretations of the Old Testament prophets) are still being taught....

"Such groups get a hearing by using copious citations from Ellen White (selected to slant to their view of things) and by criticizing the church."

Thus, new groups, all claiming to be the true promoters of the *Shepherd's Rod* messages of Victor Houteff, are still on a crusade to undermine the organized work of God. After the recent destruction by fire of the Waco compound, even more splinter groups have formed. Some believe that David Koresh was appointed by God to usher in the temporal kingdom of David, while others (who also claim to be "True Davidians") see him as a devil who went berserk and thought himself to be Christ.

But in the midst of all the confusion of many voices claiming to be the genuine promoters of the *Shepherd's Rod* message, they all do have one thing in common: they are obsessed with luring unsuspecting Seventh-day Adventists, along with their tithes and offerings, into their own particular group.

A Bold Claim by Victor Houteff

Houteff once made this remarkable claim (that has since come back many times to haunt him and his followers): "Our being, as you know, unswerving adherents of…Sister White's writings, full-fledged S.D.A.'s, we are sure that… Sister White's writings support the 'Rod' one hundred percent." *The Symbolic Code*, vol. 7, nos. 7-12 (July-December, 1941), p 5.

Can this claim be substantiated? Do the writings of Ellen G. White support Houteff's doctrines *"one hundred percent"*? If Victor Houteff had the gift of prophecy, as proponents of the *Shepherd's Rod* claim, then nothing he wrote would contradict the light that had been given through Mrs. White. We will here demonstrate that *many* of Houteff's teachings do in reality directly conflict with Mrs. White's writings.

Houteff's Teachings Examined

Victor Houteff was critical of those who used comparisons between his teachings and the writings of Mrs. White in order to expose him as a fraud. He wrote: "We are fully aware that the collocation of quotations from *The Shepherd's Rod* and the Spirit of Prophecy…makes them appear to be in direct conflict with each other. But this false appearance has been effected by isolating the statements from their contextual connections.…By the method they have used— disproving one person's writings by comparison with another's— any two books of the Bible can be made to contradict each other." *The Great Controversy Over "The Shepherd's Rod"*, pp. 20, 24. Yes, some books of the Bible can be made to contradict each other - *if* the quoted texts

John Churchill

are taken totally out of context. However, Houteff's charge is essentially that in *every case* where his writings have been compared with those of Mrs. White, things are *always* taken out of context in order to prove that his writings are not supported by the Spirit of Prophecy.

In light of the overwhelming number of examples that have been presented by dozens of Seventh-day Adventist scholars over the past sixty years which show where Houteff's doctrines are unsupported by Mrs. White's writings, we find it hard to believe that in every case the texts presented have been taken out of context. We will leave for the reader to decide if the examples offered in this article are, indeed, taken "from their contextual connections."

We should point out that following the above statement, Houteff goes on to point out a few inconsistencies in certain statements made in Sabbath School publications that contradict each other as being evidence that the Seventh-day Adventist church itself is guilty of what it accuses Houteff of being— a false teacher. Since when has the church claimed that everything that they publish is without error? Houteff, on the other hand, on August 31, 1931, sent out a circular letter in which he stated: "We must conclude that the 'Rod' contains *all* truth, or there is *no* truth in it save the quotations of truth. Therefore, if we admit one truth revealed by the 'Rod,' then we must accept *all* as truth....Therefore, we take the position that the message in the 'Rod' is free from error in so far as the idea put forth is concerned." He repeated that statement in 1935, and reaffirmed it in 1947. [See V. T. Houteff, *The Symbolic Code*, vol. 1, no. 8 (Feb15, 1935), p 1; and *Timely Greetings*, vol. 1, no. 18 (address of Dec 7, 1947), p 10.]

The Little Armageddon

Houteff claimed that his writings contained *"all* truth" and were "free from error." Some critics believe Houteff was claiming that his writings were *infallible*. Others would say that he was merely asserting that his writings contained no heresy. We will give Mr. Houteff the benefit of the doubt and say that he truly believed his writings did not blatantly contradict any light that God had revealed to his prophet Ellen White. Let us examine several of Victor Houteff's teachings to see if his writings are in harmony with what the Lord revealed to Mrs. White.

Perfect Safety

Davidians teach that a passage of Scripture found in Isaiah 11:6-9 proves that genuine followers of the *Shepherd's Rod* will remain in perfect safety during the time referred to as the Great Time of Trouble. The passage in Isaiah reads thus: "The wolf shall also dwell with the lamb, and the leopard shall lie down with the kid; and the calf and the young lion and the fatling together; and a little child shall lead them. And the cow and the bear shall feed; their young ones shall lie down together: and the lion shall eat straw like the ox. And the suckling child shall play on the hole of the asp, and the weaned child shall put his hand on the cockatrice's den. They shall not hurt nor destroy in all My holy mountain: for the earth shall be full of the knowledge of the Lord, as the waters cover the sea."

Davidians place the scene of peace and serenity as described by Isaiah in a kingdom on this earth *before* the second coming of Christ. Houteff taught that at some point in time his followers would move to Palestine and set up an organization that would orchestrate the Loud Cry. He promised his followers that they would live in perfect safety during the time when the rest of the world was going through the dreaded Time of Trouble.

Did Ellen White write anything about Isaiah 11:6-9 that would support Houteff's assertion? Here is her commentary on what Isaiah wrote: **"Those who accept the teachings of God's word will not be wholly ignorant concerning the heavenly abode. And yet, 'eye hath not seen, nor ear heard, neither have entered into the heart of man, the things which God hath prepared for them that love Him.' 1 Corinthians 2:9. Human language is inadequate to describe the reward of the righteous. It will be known only to those who behold it. No finite mind can comprehend the glory of the Paradise of God.**

"In the Bible the inheritance of the saved is called a country. There the heavenly Shepherd leads His flock to fountains of living waters. 'My people shall dwell in a peaceable habitation, and is sure dwellings, and in quiet resting places....' The wolf also shall dwell with the lamb, and the leopard shall lie down with the kid... and a little child shall lead them.' 'They shall not hurt nor destroy in all My holy mountain,' saith the Lord." *The Great Controversy*, pp. 75, 676.

The scene that the Bible portrays in Isaiah 11 is presented by Houteff as being in a kingdom on this earth *prior to the return of Christ*, while that very same scene is said by Mrs. White to portray the "*heavenly abode.*" Will you believe Houteff or Mrs. White?

A staunch defender of Davidian doctrine once told me that Seventh-day Adventists are "obsessed with Time of Trouble" and are overly worried about how terrible it will be for the elect of God during that time. It is true that many Seventh-day Adventists are very concerned about what God's people must go through during the Time of Trouble, and those concerns are based on the writings of a true prophet. Mrs. White wrote many vivid descriptions of what the people of God must endure. The following passage is from the chapter in the book *The Great Controversy* titled "The Time Of Trouble": "The people of God will not be free from suffering; but while persecuted and distressed, while they endure privation and suffer for want of food they will not be left to perish." (page 629). Ellen White revealed that the Time of Trouble would be "a time of fearful agony" for God's people. (*Ibid*, page 630.)

In another description of what the people of God must endure during the Time of Trouble, Mrs. White described how many "will be cast into the most unjust and cruel bondage" and how "the beloved of God pass weary days, bound in chains, shut in by prison bars, sentenced to be slain, some apparently left to die of starvation in dark and loathsome dungeons." (*Ibid*, page 626.) Do those scenes portray God's people dwelling in perfect safety during the Time of Trouble? Contrast these scenes that Mrs. White portrayed with Houteff's scene of the lamb and the leopard lying down with the kid, and the calf and the young lion scampering around together. Mrs. White wrote of the persecution, the distress, the cruel bondage, and the privation and hunger which lies in store for those who remain loyal to God when the rest of the world turns against them. Houteff, on the other hand, misapplied Isaiah's description of the heavenly abode to lure his followers into a sense of false security, assuring them they would dwell in perfect safety during the Time of Trouble.

One final point about Houteff's attempt to assure his followers that they would escape from the trials and sufferings of the

Time of Trouble. The popular doctrine of the "Rapture" as taught by the nominal Protestant churches is just another version of the same idea--that God's true followers will be spared from suffering through the Time of Jacob's Trouble by being "raptured" up to heaven prior to that time. But whether the theory presents the saints as being raptured to heaven *prior* to the Time of Trouble, or dwelling in Palestine as described in Isaiah 11 *during* the time when the world is in the throws of the last great conflict, a false sense of security is established in the minds of those who have been taken in by the lie.

When Will Christ Set Up His Kingdom And Rule On The Throne?

The cornerstone of Davidian doctrine is the idea that God will set up His kingdom prior to the close of probation, and that the throne of David will be established in Palestine upon which a "man" (who is *not* Christ) will sit to "judge" and "seek judgment." Remove that cornerstone doctrine, and the rest of Houteff's doctrines will topple.

How does the theory that God will establish a kingdom on earth prior to the close of probation stand in comparison to what Mrs. White wrote on the subject of Christ's throne? Houteff claimed this novel idea of the throne being set up before the return of Jesus was "new light" that God had shown him, but is it supported by light that had already been revealed prior to Houteff's arrival on the scene? The following light revealed in the inspired writings of Ellen White will answer the question: **"Not until the personal advent of Christ can His people receive the kingdom. The Saviour said: 'When the Son of man shall come in His glory, and all the holy angels with Him, then shall He sit upon the throne of His glory: and before Him** shall be gathered all nations: and He shall separate them one from another, as a shepherd divideth his sheep from the goats….Paul says: 'Flesh and blood cannot inherit the kingdom of God…' 1 Corinthians 15:50. Man in his present state is mortal, corruptible; but the kingdom of God will be incorruptible, enduring forever. Therefore man in his present state cannot enter into the kingdom of God. But when Jesus comes, He confers immortality upon His people; and then He calls them to inherit the kingdom of which they have hitherto been only heirs."** *The Great Controversy*, pp. 322, 323.

In no uncertain terms, the Holy Spirit has revealed that "*Not until the personal advent of Christ can His people receive the kingdom.*" Houteff, in plain opposition to this revealed light, claimed that the kingdom would be set up, not only before "the personal advent of Christ," but even before probation closes.

Further evidence that Mrs. White's writings do not support this particular idea of Houteff's may be found in this quote: **"So the throne of glory represents the kingdom of glory; and this kingdom is referred to in the Savior's words: 'When the Son of man shall come in His glory, and all the holy angels with Him, *then* shall He sit on the throne of His glory….' Matthew 25:31. This kingdom is yet future. It is not to be set up until the second advent of Christ."** *The Great Controversy*, p. 347.

Note the contradiction: Houteff taught that the establishment of Christ's throne will be before the close of probation; but Mrs. White revealed that **"Not until the personal advent of Christ can His people receive the kingdom"** and **"When the Son of man shall come in His glory, and all**

the holy angels with Him, *then* shall He sit on the throne of His glory."

Houteff went to great lengths to build upon his idea that the kingdom of God would be set up prior to the return of Jesus, and as he built his theory, he added the idea that since the throne of the kingdom is set up before Christ returns, then one must conclude that the person who sits on the throne is not Jesus but a real "man." Has it not always been the intention of Satan to sit on God's throne and be worshipped? We know from the apostle Paul that a "man" will try to sit in the place of God, and that man is the pope— the antichrist. No man but the Man Christ Jesus has the right to sit on Christ's throne as a judge.

The New Covenant - Yet To Come or Already In Existence?

This next example is one in which the contrast between what Houteff espoused and what the inspired pen of Ellen White clearly revealed is blatant. Houteff taught that the old covenant is the only covenant that has to this day existed, and that the new covenant is yet to be fulfilled. Here is what he taught on this matter: "The old 'covenant' or agreement between God and His people was upon the promises of both parties based thus [then he quotes the old covenant as written in Exodus 19:8 and Deuteronomy 28:1-9].

"The above paragraph describes the first covenant, which covers the period from the time it was made to the imminent and final ingathering of the twelve tribes as a kingdom, and which covenant has been broken by the Old and the New Testament churches until this very day....But the covenant, which the Lord is now about to make, is to be unlike the old. The commandments of God (Exod 20:1-17) will not be written on tables of stone (Exod 31:18), but 'in fleshly tables of the heart,' and at that time all shall 'know the Lord….'

"This is the second covenant, which God is about to make, and the law of God, being written on the heart, will be perfectly kept; then, and not before, will the blessings, which His ancient people failed to realize, be fully ours." *Tract 8*, pp. 68-70.

Right away one sees the hidden meaning of this theory, which has been the accusation of Satan since the beginning of the Great Controversy - that the law of God cannot be kept. Houteff's teaching of the two covenants leads to the conclusion that people are incapable of keeping God's law, and that we must wait for some future day for that to happen.

Did Mrs. White agree with Houteff's assertion that the new covenant, which enables a person to keep God's law, is yet to be fulfilled? Her testimony regarding this matter is this: **"As the Bible presents two laws, one changeless and eternal, the other provisional and temporary, so there are two covenants. The covenant of grace was first made with man in Eden, when after the Fall, there was given a divine promise that the seed of the woman should bruise the serpent's head. To all men this covenant offered pardon and the assisting grace of God for future obedience through faith in Christ. It also promised them eternal life on condition of fidelity to God's law. Thus the patriarchs received the hope of salvation….**

"Another compact - called in Scripture the 'old' covenant - was formed between God and Israel at Sinai, and was then ratified by the blood of a sacrifice. The Abrahamic covenant was ratified by the blood of Christ, and it is

called the 'second,' or 'new,' covenant, because the blood by which it was sealed was shed after the blood of the first covenant. That the new covenant was valid in the days of Abraham is evident from the fact that it was then confirmed both by the promise and the oath of God...." *Patriarchs & Prophets*, pp. 370, 371.

"Every time a soul is converted, and learns to love God and keep His commandments, the promise of God is fulfilled, 'A new heart also will I give you, and a new spirit will I put in you.'" *The Desire of Ages*, p 407.

Houteff asserted that the new covenant is one that God is "*about* to make" (that it is still *future*), but the Spirit of Prophecy teaches us that **"the new covenant was valid in the days of Abraham"** and that **"Every time a soul is converted...the promise of God is *fulfilled*, 'A new heart also will I give you, and a new spirit will I put in you."**

Another Subtle Heresy Taught By Houteff

Seventh-day Adventists have been accused by nominal Protestants of elevating Mrs. White's writings to the same level as the Holy Scriptures. That, of course, is a false claim; for we view Mrs. White's writings to be an inspired commentary of the Word of God, but they are not to supercede Scripture. One thing is certain, however, and that is that Ellen White never made the assertion that we can obtain a true knowledge of the Bible only through her writings. Can the same thing be said of Victor Houteff?

In Zechariah 4:1-6 and 12-14, Zechariah was wakened from sleep by an angel and saw a golden candlestick, a bowl on top of it, and "seven lamps thereon, and seven pipes to the seven lamps." He also saw two olive trees (or branches), one on the right and one on the left, from which oil passed through two golden pipes. He asked the angel what the branches and pipes were, and the angel said that "These are the two anointed ones, that stand by the Lord of the whole earth."

Now let us see what application Houteff gave to this scene. He wrote: "The two pipes through which the oil is carried into the bowl, can only represent the channels (prophets) through whom the oil is transferred from the Bible into the bowl, in the period during which both olive trees (Old and New Testaments) live - in the Christian era.

"Let the reader take a searching look at the visual illustration on page 19 [of his tract], and he will see the utter impossibility of he candlestick's (the church membership's) and of the tubes' (ministers') themselves, extracting oil direct from the olive trees. The interpretation of the Scriptures, therefore, being entrusted to the two pipes (prophets) in the Christian Era shows that 'no prophecy of the Scriptures is of any private interpretation,' but is of inspiration only....

"The interpreters (the two golden pipes), therefore, are the only ones who are enabled to bring forth meat in due season (golden oil) from the Scriptures (olive trees) into the storehouse (golden bowl) of present truth, and by the aid of the ministers (seven tubes) to pass on the oil to the church (candlestick), that it might illumine with the light of life this dark and dying world of ours." *Tract 6*, revised, pp. 23,24.

Did you catch the subtle insinuation in Houteff's explanation of the scene in Zechariah? He tried to convey the "utter impossibility" of God's people and even the ministers of obtaining a true knowledge of the Bible except as received through God's prophets.

How does this claim of Houteff fair in comparison to what Mrs. White had to say? She wrote in regards to the same scene in Zechariah: **"The continued communication of the Holy Spirit to the church is represented by the prophet Zechariah under another figure, which contains a wonderful lesson of encouragement for us....From the two olives trees, the golden oil was emptied through golden pipes into the bowl of the candlestick and thence into the golden lamps that gave light to the sanctuary. So from the holy ones that stand in God's presence, His Spirit is imparted to human instrumentalities that are consecrated to His service. The mission of the two anointed ones is to communicate light and power to God's people. It is to receive the blessing for us that they stand in God's presence. As the olive trees empty themselves into the golden pipes, so the heavenly messengers seek to communicate all that they receive from God. The whole heavenly treasure awaits our demand and reception; and as we receive the blessing, we in turn are to impart it. Thus it is that the holy lamps are fed, and the church becomes a light bearer in the world.**

"This is the work that the Lord would have every soul prepared to do at this time....We should daily receive the holy oil, that we may impart to others....From the two olive trees the golden oil flowing through the golden pipes has been communicated to us." *Testimonies To Ministers*, 509-511.

Is it clear whom the two pipes represent? **"Let every man who enters the pulpit know that he has *angels from heaven* in his audience. And when these *angels* empty from themselves the golden oil of truth into the heart of him who is teaching the word, then the application of the truth will be a solemn, serious matter."** *Testimonies*

To Ministers, p 338. The two pipes represent the *holy angels* who bring the truths of God's word directly to "the heart of him who is teaching the word," whether that person is a minister or a layman sharing the Word with others who wish to discover Bible truth.

Remember, we are establishing the fact that Victor Houteff claimed that he had the gift of prophecy. He even went so far as to claim that it is impossible for people to understand the Bible aside from his interpretation of Scripture. In an official publication of the Davidian SDAs, the claim is made that "the prophetic gift in the Seventh-day Adventist church (through the medium of which the church was brought forth in 1844 and nurtured and preserved for seven decades) ceased its manifestation in 1915 [upon the death of Ellen White] and was not remanifested until 1930…." *Fundamental Beliefs and Directory of The Davidian Seventh-day Adventists*, 1943, pp. 11,12. Of course, 1930 was when Houteff began writing his *Shepherd's Rod* messages.

Hazel Hendricks, who beginning in 1933 was a follower of Victor Houteff for seven years, but who later came to see the error in his teachings, authored a booklet where she wrote: "The author of the Shepherd's Rod would convey the thought to God's people that they can obtain knowledge of the Scriptures only through him. According to his teachings on this very point, the thought he wishes to convey in his tract is that the two pipes represent Mrs. E. G. White and himself; and as Mrs. White is dead, that leaves *him* to communicate the 'oil' to the church." *The True Witness Speaks: The Teachings of The Shepherd's Rod in the Light of the Bible and the Spirit of Prophecy*, p 10.

Was the Spirit of Prophecy manifested in the writings of Victor Houteff? When God was establishing Ellen White as His special messenger, plenty of evidence was provided that pointed to her special gift. It is common knowledge that Mrs. White would be taken off in vision during public meetings where the gift could be witnessed even by skeptics. All present could verify the supernatural manifestations that accompanied her visions (loss of breath, no eye-blinking, supernatural strength, etc.). Over a period of several years, the evidence that Mrs. White possessed the prophetic gift was too overwhelming to deny.

Does V. T. Houteff meet the tests of a Bible prophet? Where has it ever been established that he also possessed the gift of prophecy? He never acknowledged that *visions* and *dreams* - God's appointed methods of revealing light to His prophets - were the ways through which he received special "light" from the Lord. Houteff, in fact, claimed that the "light" he received from God came to him through several years of Bible study.

The Spirit of prophecy is filled with warnings to avoid those individuals who constantly arise claiming that God has sent them with "new light" to give to the church. This is not to say that there is no more light to receive; but if gross error is to be found in that which is called "new light," then it must be rejected. Houteff, whose writings contained multiple errors, *insisted* that he had the prophetic gift and that all Seventh-day Adventists *must* accept his teachings or be destroyed. But he is only one of many individuals who fulfilled Mrs. White's prediction that **"Men who want to present something original will conjure up things new and strange, and without consideration will step forward on these unstable theories, that have been woven together as a precious theory, and present it as a life and death question."** *Selected Messages, Book Two*, p 15.

The Little Armageddon

Does The Mount of Olives Split Twice?

The Davidian SDA people claim to believe in the inspiration of Ellen White, but we have shown that Mrs. White's writings do not support the idea that the kingdom of God will be set up in Palestine prior to the close of probation. Houteff was once asked why he believed that the scene described in Zechariah 14:4, which describes the Lord descending on the Mount of Olives, took place before the close of probation. He was shown that Mrs. White wrote that this scene described the New Jerusalem descending *after* the close of the thousand years. His answer was that what Sister White wrote was right, but that hers was a "secondary application." His explanation of the text was the primary application which was the setting up of the throne prior to the close of probation. He did not offer an explanation as to how the Mount of Olives could be twice split asunder and become a "very great valley."

As previously stated, if the doctrine of setting up the kingdom of David in Jerusalem prior to the close of probation is proved to be false, then the rest of the *Shepherd's Rod* doctrine comes crashing down. Obviously, Mrs. White never received such a teaching from God, for as we have already noted, she once wrote: **"A line of truth extending from that time** [when our church pioneers hammered out our distinct doctrines] **to the time when we shall enter the city of God, was made plain to me."** Series B, No. 2, p. 57. In that "line of truth," she saw the Loud Cry, the Sunday Law, the Time of Trouble, the seven last plagues, the second coming, and all the other major events that took place up to the time when the redeemed enter the city of God. It is inconceivable that God left out of that time line such an important event as the setting up of a temporal kingdom in old Palestine where a throne would be established upon which would sit a finite man in the place of the living Christ.

Ezekiel 9

No discussion of the Davidian SDA organization would be complete without examining their interpretation of Ezekiel chapter 9. The basic teaching of Houteff was that any Seventh-day Adventist who rejects the Shepherd's Rod message will be destroyed by angels wielding swords, and that the slaughter will take place prior to the Loud Cry and the close of probation. Does his interpretation of Ezekiel 9 find support in Mrs. White's writings? Let's find out.

Houteff wrote this concerning Ezekiel 9: "According to Ezekiel 2:3; 3:1,4,5,7, the prophet was to bear his message to the whole 'house of Israel....' Yet he did not understand the meaning of the vision....

"Since at the time of the vision, the house of Judah, the two-tribe kingdom, was in captivity in the land of the Chaldeans, and the house of Israel, the ten-tribe kingdom, was in dispersion among the nations whither it had been carried away and scattered some years before (2 Kings 17:6), there was no possibility of Ezekiel's delivering the message to them. And as it is to both the house of Israel and the house of Judah (Ezekiel 9:9), - the twelve tribes - consequently it was prophetic in Ezekiel's time....

"And finally as no slaughter such as the one described in Ezekiel 9 has ever occurred, its fulfillment is obviously yet future." *Tract 1*, pp.11,12, second revised edition.

Houteff here makes three astonishing statements: (1) that Ezekiel did not understand the meaning of the message he was to deliver; (2) that he did not take the message to whom he was told to deliver it; and (3) that the slaughter foretold has never occurred, and must therefore be a future event. Let us turn to the Spirit of Prophecy to see if Mrs. White supported these three statements.

Mrs. White wrote concerning the prophet Ezekiel: **"While Jeremiah continued to bear his testimony in the land of Judah, the prophet Ezekiel was raised up from among the captives in Babylon, to warn and to comfort the exiles, and also to confirm the word of the Lord that was being spoken through Jeremiah. During the years that remained of Zedekiah's reign, Ezekiel made very plain the folly of trusting to the false predictions of those who were causing the captives to hope for an early return to Jerusalem. He was also instructed to foretell, by means of a variety of symbols and solemn messages, the siege and utter destruction of Jerusalem."**

"In the sixth year of the reign of Zedekiah, the Lord revealed to Ezekiel in vision some of the abominations that were being practiced in Jerusalem, and within the gate of the Lord's house, and even in the inner court. The chambers of images, and the pictured idols, 'every form of creeping things, and abominable beasts, and all the idols of the house of Israel'— all these in rapid succession passed before the astonished gaze of the prophet. Ezekiel 8:10.

"Those who should have been spiritual leaders among the people, 'the ancients of the house of Israel,' to the number of seventy, were seen offering incense before the idolatrous representations that had been introduced into hidden chambers within the sacred precincts of the temple court....

"And now the glorious Being who accompanied Ezekiel throughout this astonishing vision of the wickedness in high places in the land of Judah, inquired of the prophet: 'Hast thou seen this, O son of man? Is it a light thing to the house of Judah that they commit the abominations which they commit here? For they have filled the land with violence, and have returned to provoke Me in anger...Therefore I will also deal in fury: Mine eyes shall not spare, neither will I have pity: and though they cry in Mine ears with a loud voice, yet will I not hear them' (verses 17, 18)....

"The day of doom for the kingdom of Judah was fast approaching. No longer could the Lord set before them hope of averting the severest of His judgments. 'Should ye be utterly unpunished?' He inquired. 'Ye shall not be unpunished.'

"Even these words were received with mocking derision.... 'Tell them,' the Lord declared,...I will speak, and the word that I shall speak shall come to pass; it shall be no more prolonged: for in your days, O rebellious house, will I say the word, and perform it, saith the Lord God.'" *Prophets & Kings*, 448-450.

How thankful we are that the Lord gave us the Spirit of Prophecy so that we may have a divine commentary on Scripture. The above words of Ellen White reveal the three theories of Houteff regarding Ezekiel to be groundless.

The first of Houteff's claims was that Ezekiel did not understand the meaning of the message he was to deliver. He concludes that because Ezekiel was "astonished," that meant he did not understand the vision. Yet the inspired commentary declared that the message God gave to Ezekiel was to **"warn and to comfort the exiles,"** to make **"very plain the folly of trusting to the false predictions of those who were causing the captives to hope for an early return to Jerusalem," "to foretell, by means of a variety of symbols and solemn messages, the siege and utter destruction of Jerusalem"** and all the reasons why God was going to destroy the city, such as the spiritual leaders **"offering incense before the idolatrous representations that had been introduced into hidden chambers within the sacred precincts of the temple court."** From this we can see that Ezekiel definitely understood the content of the message he was sent to deliver. The Spirit of Prophecy does *not* support the assertion put forth by Houteff that Ezekiel "did not understand the meaning of the vision."

The second claim of Houteff was that Ezekiel did not take the message to whom he was told to deliver it to. The Bible itself states in Ezekiel 2:3, "I send thee to the children of Israel, to a rebellious nation." Where is the evidence that Ezekiel did not fulfill that commission? Mrs. White wrote that **"the prophet Ezekiel was *raised up*"** for the very purpose of *warning* and comforting the exiles; and that Ezekiel's warnings **"were received with mocking derision."** How could the people *receive* the words of warning if Ezekiel never told them?

And the final claim of Houteff was that the slaughter foretold has never occurred. He wrests from its true meaning the text which said the vision "is for many days to come, and he prophesieth of the times that are afar off." But the Lord asserted: "Thus saith the Lord God: There shall *none of my words be prolonged any more*, but the word which I have spoken shall be done." (chapter 12:27, 28)

Bible historians and the Spirit of Prophecy agree that Jerusalem was destroyed in fulfillment of Ezekiel's prophecy when Nebuchadnezzar marched his armies into Jerusalem, destroyed the city and slaughtered the Jews. Houteff misapplied the "sword" spoken of in Ezekiel 21:3 to mean a literal sword. The Lord said, "Thus saith the Lord, behold I am against thee, and will draw forth My sword out of his sheath"; and again in verses 9 and 10, "A sword, a sword is sharpened, and also furbished: it is sharpened to make a sore slaughter." This is where Houteff got the notion that God would send angels to slaughter with a sword Seventh-day Adventists who rejected the *Shepherd's Rod* message; and every Shepherd's Rod splinter group to this day believes in Houteff's fanciful theory.

The predictions of Ezekiel were predictions that Jerusalem would be destroyed for their great wickedness, and Seventh-day Adventists have always taught that the armies of Babylon were the agencies that God (or the "sword") used to accomplish this punishment of His people.

The Lord told Ezekiel that the punishment would be in "times that are afar off," but He also qualified that time by saying that the fulfillment would not "be prolonged any more." The prophecy was not fulfilled immediately, but it was fulfilled in Ezekiel's lifetime. The Lord told Ezekiel that an eyewitness who would escape the destruction would give him an account of the destruction: "He that escapeth in that day shall come unto thee, to cause thee to hear it with thine ears [that the city was destroyed]." Ezekiel 24:26.

To clear up any final doubt that the destruction of Jerusalem in Ezekiel's day by the armies of Babylon was the fulfillment of the vision given to Ezekiel, we offer this inspired comment of Mrs. White: **"In the ninth year of Zedekiah's reign,**

'Nebuchadnezzar king of Babylon came, he, and all his host, against Jerusalem,' to besiege the city. The outlook for Judah was hopeless. 'Behold, I am against thee,' the Lord Himself declared through Ezekiel. 'I the Lord have *drawn forth My sword* out of his sheath: it shall not return anymore...I will pour out Mine indignation upon thee, I will blow against thee in the fire of My wrath, and deliver thee into the hand of brutish men, and skillful to destroy' (Ezekiel 21:3, 5-7, 31)." *Prophets & Kings*, p. 452.

Mrs. White did apply the destruction of Jerusalem both in Ezekiel's day and in the year 70 AD to the general destruction of the wicked in the last days. **"In the destruction of the impenitent city we see a symbol of the final destruction of the world."** This destruction is applied to the "world" and not just to unfaithful Seventh-day Adventists. And we know that this destruction will come by means other than by a literal sword wielded by angels.

The Davidian SDAs teach that there will be a literal slaughter of Seventh-day Adventists who reject their message, and that the slaughter will take place *prior* to the Loud Cry. Yet the Spirit of Prophecy teaches that disloyal Seventh-day Adventists will *leave* the church during the Great Shaking and join the ranks of the enemy. There they will perish along with the rest of the wicked, being destroyed, not by sword-wielding angels, but by the seven last plagues and by the brightness of Christ's glory when He returns to rescue His loyal followers.

One Davidian group has released an audio tape which is a study of Zechariah chapter 6. On the tape the speaker reads an Ellen White quote (found in *Testimonies* Volume 3) which deals with the sealing of the 144,000. His goal is to convince his listeners that unsealed Seventh-day Adventists will be destroyed in a separate destruction than that of non-believers who are outside the church. In the quote the speaker read from *Testimonies* Volume 3, Mrs. White contrasted the "true people of God" with those in the church who "excuse wrongs" and "murmur in their hearts…against those who would reprove sin." She explains that the "figure of each man having a slaughter weapon in his hand" (as described in Ezekiel 9) is shown to be symbolic of the destruction of those Seventh-day Adventists who do not repent and receive the seal of God. No problem so far. We totally agree with Davidians who say that angels in Ezekiel 9 who have slaughter weapons (swords) are symbolic of the fact that God will destroy unfaithful Seventh-day Adventists some day.

But, regarding the destruction of those unfaithful church members, we ask this question: *When* will they "fall"? Ellen White declared that they "will fall in the general destruction of the wicked, represented by the work of the five men bearing slaughter weapon." *Testimonies*, Vol. 3, pp. 266, 267. The point we are about to establish is of critical importance, for it illustrates more clearly than any of the arguments put forth so far in this article that Houteff's teachings contradict the teachings of Ellen White concerning major events that will occur prior to the end of time.

Mrs. White puts the "fall" of unsealed church members at the time of "the general destruction of the wicked." Make sure that you understand this point before going on. We are talking about *when* unfaithful Seventh-day Adventists will be destroyed. Davidians teach that unsealed Adventists will be destroyed *before* the Loud Cry, which comes before the close of probation. But Mrs. White places their destruction at the time of "the general destruction of the wicked." And the general destruction of the wicked does not happen until *after* the Loud Cry and *after* the close of probation. The wicked non-believers will be destroyed by the seven last plagues and not by the destroying angels of Ezekiel 9. It is only logical to conclude that if unfaithful Seventh-day Adventists are destroyed at the same time as "the general destruction of the wicked," then they will also be destroyed by the plagues, which occurs during the time of the "general destruction of the wicked." Our Davidian friends would have us take a literal interpretation of Ezekiel chapter 9; but Mrs. White wrote clearly that "They [the unsealed Adventists] will fall in the general destruction of the wicked, represented by the work of the five men bearing slaughter weapons." Note the use of the word "represented" in the above quote. The "five men bearing slaughter weapons" in Ezekiel 9 is a representation of what will occur during the time of the general destruction of the wicked--it is symbolic of that event. There is nothing in the writings of Ellen White that makes that time of slaughter apply to a special time of destruction that occurs before the close of probation. To accept the Davidian teaching on this matter would be to defy all logic.

Yet the Davidian speaker on the sermon tape goes to great lengths to try and convince his listeners that the general destruction of the wicked and the slaughter of unsealed Seventh-day Adventists are two different events at two different times. He would have us believe that unsealed church members fall not only before probation closes, but even before the Loud Cry. The rest of the wicked, he says, fall in the plagues after probation closes. Yet, with all his verbal footwork, he is still faced with the fact that Mrs. White put the "fall" of unfaithful Seventh-day Adventist church members at a single time and event, which she calls "the general destruction of the wicked." And that event will take place after probation closes.

Contrasting the Davidian doctrine of the destruction of unsealed church members with what the Spirit of Prophecy actually teaches on the subject is important, for it perfectly illustrates how Davidians distort the Spirit of Prophecy to make it say what they want it to say. They quote Mrs. White, then seek to undo what she wrote by offering private interpretations of various Bible symbols and texts, which end up being nothing less than fanciful interpretations that have no basis whatsoever in logic or upon sound theological principles.

Much more could be said about the wrong interpretations of Victor Houteff regarding Ezekiel 9, but we must go on to other topics. Those who wish to further study the subject of Ezekiel 9 as contrasted between V. T. Houteff's theories and the writings of Mrs. White should call or write the General Conference of Seventh-day Adventists and request the pamphlet written by Hazel Hendricks titled *The True Witness Speaks: The Teachings of the Shepherd's Rod in the Light of the Bible and the Spirit of Prophecy.*

Those who now embrace the *Shepherd's Rod* message will someday witness the Loud Cry taking place and wonder why the slaughter did not occur. Perhaps some will open their eyes at that time, give up their false ideas, and come over to the true remnant church.

Who Are The 144,000?

It has already been pointed out that Davidian SDAs seek to mingle amongst Seventh-day Adventists. They have been known to move to a particular location (especially where they can find a group of Adventists in the process of

The Little Armageddon

establishing a new church congregation) and get themselves on the membership roll. Then they begin to share their "new light" with anyone who will listen.

Is there any way to spot a Davidian SDA amongst traditional Seventh-day Adventists? There are many Davidian groups claiming to be the true followers of the *Shepherd's Rod* and each have their own unique brand of doctrine and practice. Since there are so many different beliefs amongst all the Davidian groups, it can be somewhat difficult to find common denominators to help identify someone as a Davidian. In general, however, there are a few clues to look for that a person might be a Davidian. Not all, but many Davidians (1) drop to their knees when anyone prays; (2) never places their tithe or offerings into the offering plate in a Seventh-day Adventist Church; and (3) believe that women *must* wear a hat in the sanctuary. At least one group of Davidians now refers to Christ as "Yahshua" and believes that Sabbath-keepers must also keep all of the annual feasts such as the Feast of Tabernacles and the Day of Pentecost. But there is one subject they all do seem to have very much in common, and that is their strange fascination with the subject of the 144,000.

Many Seventh-day Adventists are confused as to who make up the 144,000, and for that reason, many are lured into studying this subject with Davidian SDAs. Some who have never studied the subject thoroughly are charmed by the picture of the 144,000 as painted by the Davidian Adventists. Therefore, Davidians often use this subject as their opening wedge into the minds of unsuspecting Seventh-day Adventists.

Davidian SDAs believe that the 144,000 will be the sealed, sinless, and safe inhabitants of that perfect kingdom of

David to be set up in the Holy Land prior to the close of probation. Therefore, they teach that the identity of those who make up the 144,000 will be known *before* the close of probation and that they will assume control of the "church militant" and will finish the work of God.

This is in contrast to Mrs. White's understanding that the 144,000 will be those who occupy a special place in the heavenly abode, having suffered through the Time of Trouble and triumphed over the beast and its image. Nowhere in the writings of Ellen White is it found or even implied that the identity of the 144,000 will be revealed before the close of probation, much less that this group would occupy the Holy Land and from their headquarters direct the activities of the Loud Cry.

John the Revelator saw in vision a scene of the 144,000 standing upon Mount Zion. He described the vision this way: "Then I looked, and behold, a Lamb standing on Mount Zion, and with Him one hundred and forty-four thousand, having His Father's name written on their foreheads." Revelation 14:1. NKJV.

Referring to this vision, Houteff wrote: "Let it be carefully noted that in his vision, John saw the 144,000 stand not on Mount Zion in heaven, but upon earth, for had it not been otherwise, he would not say 'I heard a voice from heaven.'.... In view of the fact that the 144,000 stood on Mount Zion while the elders and the beasts were before the throne, the 144,000 were, therefore, sealed while the judgment was in session. Moreover, Christ being seen with them in His symbolical form (a lamb), again proves that they stand with Him on Mount Zion during the probationary time— while the judgment is in session." *Tract 8*, p 4,6,7.

The Little Armageddon

Note that Houteff places this vision of John on the earth (although the logic he uses to establish this theory is highly suspect). Contrast his theory of the scene taking place on earth with the following light on the subject of the 144,000 as revealed by God's true prophet: **"In holy vision the prophet saw the ultimate triumph of God's remnant church. He writes:**

"'I saw as it were a sea of glass mingled with fire: and them that had gotten the victory...stand on the sea of glass, having the harps of God. And they sing the song of Moses the servant of God, and the song of the Lamb....' Revelation 15:2,3.

"'And I looked, and, lo, a Lamb stood on the Mount Sion, and with Him a hundred and forty and four thousand, having His Father's name written in their foreheads.' Revelation 14:1. In this world their minds were consecrated to God; they served Him with the intellect and with the heart; and now He can place His name 'in their foreheads....'

"'These are they which follow the Lamb whithersoever He goeth. These were the redeemed from among men, being the first fruits unto God and to the Lamb.' Revelation 14:4. The vision of the prophet pictures them as standing on Mount Zion, girt for holy service, clothed in white linen, which is the righteousness of the saints. But all who follow the Lamb in heaven must first have followed Him on earth, not fretfully or capriciously, but in trustful, loving, willing obedience, as the flock follows the shepherd.

"'I heard the voice of harpers harping with their harps: and they sung as it were a new song before the throne:...

and no man could learn that song but the hundred and forty and four thousand, which were redeemed from the earth....In their mouth was found no guile: for they are without fault before the throne of God.'" *Acts of the Apostles*, pp 590,591.

Note that she places the vision of John, not on earth, but at the time of the "ultimate triumph of God's remnant church." That time of ultimate triumph comes *after* the return of Christ when the redeemed are taken to the city, wherein is the "sea of glass." In order to make this vision appear to take place on earth, Houteff had to invent the idea that there still remains *two* returns of Jesus— an *invisible* one wherein the 144,000 will be sealed when the temporal kingdom is set up in Palestine, and a visible return during which the 144,000 and the ones they ushered into the kingdom (the great multitude) are translated without seeing death.

More evidence may be presented from the pen of Ellen White that places the 144,000 in heaven: **"While John was shown the last great struggles of the church with earthly powers, he was also permitted to behold the final victory and deliverance of the faithful. He saw the church brought into deadly conflict with the beast and his image** [note the contrast here to the idea of living in perfect safety at headquarters in Palestine], **and the worship of that beast enforced on pain of death. But looking beyond the smoke and din of the battle, he beheld a company upon Mount Zion with the Lamb, having, instead of the mark of the beast, the 'Father's' name written in their foreheads.'"** *Testimonies*, vol. 5, pp. 752, 753.

How clear it is that John's vision looked "beyond the smoke and din of the battle" that took place in the struggle against the beast and its image, on to the heavenly scene which John described in Revelation 14:1, the scene that Houteff places on this earth and not in heaven.

Mrs. White, describing a scene she saw in vision, wrote: **"We all entered the cloud together, and were seven days ascending to the sea of glass, when Jesus brought the crowns, and with His own right hand placed them on our heads. He gave us harps of gold and palms of victory. Here on the sea of glass the 144,000 stood in a perfect square."** *Ibid.*, vol. 1, pp. 60, 61.

Note that they *ascended* to the sea of glass, which is where John saw the 144,000. To ascend means to *go up*— to ascend up into the cloud of angels that accompany Jesus when He returns. From there the redeemed are taken off to heaven, and there it is that John saw the 144,000 standing on the sea of glass.

Mrs. White described the 144,000 who stood on the sea of glass as those who will be **"translated from the earth, from among the living....These are they which came out of great tribulation; they have endured the anguish of the time of Jacob's trouble."** *The Great Controversy*, p. 648.

To summarize, the important point is that the 144,000 will not acquire their status as first fruits until they shall have "been translated from the earth." Far from the group presented by Houteff as living in safety in Palestine and directing the conversion of the "great multitude," the 144,000's experience will include having gotten the victory over the beast, his image, mark and number; and being translated from among the living after enduring the *anguish* (extreme anxiety or emotional torment) of the time of Jacob's trouble.

The 144,000 will not take charge of the church militant, as taught by the Davidian SDA's. The view that has always been held by Seventh-day Adventists is that the 144,000 will serve God in His heavenly temple *after* the church is triumphant and safe in heaven.

In spite of the vast number of Ellen White quotes that the Davidians link together to try and prove their theory concerning the 144,000, the truth is that their ideas cannot be harmonized with the plainest of statements of Ellen White that the scene of John's vision took place in heaven and not in this old sinful world (as Houteff taught).

Oh how cautious we should be about accepting any teaching that would raise to a state of sinless perfection any person or group of persons *prior* to the close of human probation. And anyone who is entertaining the idea that an erring, finite human being will sit on *Christ's* throne before Christ Himself appears in the clouds of glory, would do well to revisit the true meaning of the term "antichrist." Only those who are *willing* to be deceived will believe that there is a human being alive today who is worthy to sit on Christ's throne in His stead. The fact that Davidian SDA's make this unbelievable claim is evidence that the spirit of antichrist is still alive and well.

Another Teaching of Houteff Contradicted By Mrs. White

Houteff taught that God did not show Enoch the truth about the flood. He wrote: "Jude proves that Enoch was a messenger of God, and yet that he warned his generation of the destruction of the world by the second advent of Christ, when, if fact, the flood was the event which was to and subsequently did destroy the world of Enoch's time! Enoch simply was not shown the truth of the flood. Therefore, he preached the destruction then in terms of the coming of Christ." *The Symbolic Code*, vol 1, no. 10 (April 15, 1935), p 9.

Mrs. White clearly differed with Houteff's claim when she wrote: **"God communed with Enoch through His angels, and gave him divine instruction. He made known to him that He would not always bear with man in his rebellion—that His purpose was to destroy the sinful race by bringing a flood of waters upon the earth."** *Spiritual Gifts*, vol. 3, p. 54. And again, **"Through holy angels, God revealed to Enoch His purpose to destroy the world by a flood…."** *Patriarchs & Prophets*, p. 85.

Houteff asserted that "Enoch simply was not shown the truth of the flood," while Mrs. White clearly taught that "God revealed to Enoch His purpose to destroy the world by a flood." Can Houteff's charge that Mrs. White's writings are always taken out of context with his own statements be substantiated in the above example? Words mean things, and the words of Houteff regarding Enoch have a meaning that is *directly opposite* to Ellen White's words. So much for his boast that "we are sure that both the Bible and Sister White's writings support the 'Rod' one hundred percent."

Fanciful Interpretations of Bible Texts

Houteff often made statements concerning various Bible texts with which he offered no proof that his interpretation was the truth.

For example: "The seven years of plenty and the seven years of famine in the days of Joseph in ancient Egypt represent the world's history in two sections of time as previously explained, namely, B.C. and A.D." *The Shepherd's Rod*, vol. 1 (1930), p. 19.

Houteff also taught the fanciful theory that the wheat mentioned in Ezekiel 4:9 is the doctrine of justification by faith as taught by Martin Luther; the barley is the doctrine concerning the Holy Spirit as taught by John Knox; the beans are the doctrine of grace as preached by John Wesley; the lentils are the doctrine of baptism by immersion as taught by Alexander Campbell; the millet is the doctrine of the 2300 days as taught by William Miller; and the spelt is the doctrine of the Sabbath in connection with the sanctuary as revealed through Ellen White. (See *The Shepherd's Rod*, vol. 1, (1930), pp. 117-120.

And where is inspired proof presented for these and other fanciful ideas that literally fill the writings of Houteff? Houteff, when confronted with that question, responded by writing: "Anyone who will take the pains to study the subject, now published in *The Shepherd's Rod*, Volume 1, will find an abundance of 'Scriptural proof.'" *The Great Controversy Over "The Shepherd's Rod"*, p. 6. So in order to confirm that a statement such as "the seven years of plenty" represents the world's history prior to the birth of Christ, one is expected to wade through vast amounts of Houteff's written material searching for the scriptural proof that such a statement is truth.

Houteff, by making such unfounded interpretations of Scripture, surely fits the description of Mrs. White when she wrote: **"In order to sustain erroneous doctrines or unchristian practices, some will seize upon passages of Scripture separated from the context…With the cunning of the serpent they entrench themselves behind disconnected utterances construed to suit their carnal**

desires. Thus do they willfully pervert the word of God. Others, who have an active imagination, seize upon the figures and symbols [such as the wheat, barley, beans, etc.] **of Holy Writ, interpret them to suit their fancy, with little regard to the testimony of Scripture as its own interpreter, and then they present their vagaries as the teachings of the Bible."** *The Great Controversy*, p. 521.

Conclusion

We could go on and on giving examples of where Mrs. White's writings do *not* support Houteff's teachings. It would take a book to deal with every point of doctrinal difference that exists between the Davidian SDA's and the Seventh-day Adventist Church. And we should point out that even between the many groups who claim to be the genuine keepers of the "Rod" there is a lot of controversy over what constitutes truth. Suffice it to say that enough evidence has been presented to prove that Houteff's claim that the Writings of Mrs. White support his teachings "one hundred percent" is totally unfounded.

In spite of the claims of Victor Houteff that his teachings were never given due investigation by the leading brethren of experience, the truth of the matter is that Seventh-day Adventist scholars and theologians have repeatedly over the past sixty-plus years examined his doctrines and continue to this day to pronounce much of the content of the *Shepherd's Rod* to be heresy.

Often Davidian SDA's will search out those church members who feel like the church has betrayed them or failed to satisfy their spiritual needs, for they know that such individuals are highly motivated to find something new[12]. Thus many are unknowingly seduced into accepting the errors of the *Shepherd's Rod*.

Many who are charmed by the unique teachings of the *Shepherd's Rod* have only a surface understanding of Seventh-day Adventist doctrines. They consider themselves wise enough to discern truth from error and find the *Shepherd's Rod* material to sound plausible. But little do they realize that as they continue to read the publications of the *Shepherd's Rod*, over a period of time the thoughts and beliefs of the *Shepherd's Rod* becomes their thoughts and beliefs. Once the error has been embraced, a mountain of evidence may be presented to show that Houteff's teachings contain error, but they no longer are able to discern truth from error.

In order to break down the prejudice that Seventh-day Adventists have against Davidian SDA's, Davidians often quote the admonition of Mrs. White that **"No matter by whom light is sent, we should open our hearts to receive it with the meekness of Christ."** *Gospel Workers*, p. 301. It is good to study that which comes purporting to be new light, for to take a stubborn attitude that there is no more light to be revealed is not wise. But do not allow the Davidians to twist the real meaning of Mrs. White's counsel. Davidians would have us emphasize the word "*whom*"—"no matter by *whom* light is sent…." In other words, the insinuation is that even if someone from an offshoot organization brings us new teachings, we "should open our hearts to receive it."

The real emphasis, however, should be on the word "light"— "No matter by whom *light* is sent…." The question is: "Are

---

[12] Or someone or something to blame or someone who sympathizes with their cause.

the strange teachings of the Davidians genuine "light," or is it a mixture of truth and error? Having investigated their so-called "new light" and seen that it is out of harmony with light that has already been revealed in Scripture and the Spirit of Prophecy, one should conclude that the message of the *Shepherd's Rod* is *not* to be received.

With all that the reader has now learned about the *Shepherd's Rod* and its founder, V. T. Houteff, we offer these final statements from the pen of Ellen White which, we hope you will see, perfectly fits the Shepherd's Rod: **"He [God] is leading, not stray offshoots, not one here and one there, but a people."** *Testimonies to Ministers*, p 61. **"God has made His church on the earth a channel of light, and through it He communicates His purposes and His will. He does not give to one of His servants an experience independent of and contrary to the experience of the church itself. Neither does He give one man a knowledge of His will for the entire church, while the church…is left in darkness."** *The Acts of the Apostles*, p 163.

"There are little companies continually arising who believe that God is only with the very few, the very scattered, and their influence is to tear down and scatter that which God's servants build up. Restless minds who want to be seeing and believing something new continually are constantly rising, some in one place and some in another, all doing a special work for the enemy, yet claiming to have the truth. They stand separate from the people whom God is leading out and prospering, and through whom He is to do His great work. They are continually expressing their fears that the body of Sabbathkeepers are becoming like the world, but there are scarcely two of those whose views are in harmony. They are scattered and confused, and yet deceive

themselves so much as to think that God is especially with them. Some of these profess to have the gifts among them; but are led by the influence and teachings of these gifts to hold in doubt those upon whom God has laid the special burden of His work, and to lead off a class from the body." *Testimonies*, vol 1 pp 417,418.

"False teachers may appear to be very zealous for the work of God, and may expend means to bring their theories before the world and the church; but as they mingle error with truth [and we have established that Houteff did just that], **their message is one of deception, and will lead souls into false paths. They are to be met and opposed, not because they are bad men, but because they are teachers of falsehood, and are endeavoring to put upon falsehood the stamp of truth."** *Testimonies to Ministers*, p. 55.

Author's Note:
I have had the sad experience of losing Seventh-day Adventist friends to the Davidians. Virtually all of my friends who in the past embraced the teachings of the *Shepherd's Rod* eventually left the Davidian movement, but none have ever returned to the Seventh-day Adventist Church.

I know that rejecting truth and embracing error will destroy a person's soul; and therefore I am determined to warn unsuspecting Seventh-day Adventists about the heresy contained in the *Shepherd's Rod*.

In my study of this elusive offshoot, I have compiled a vast amount of their published material. Nothing I have ever read in Houteff's writings speaks to my soul as do the writings of Ellen White. I have read accounts of persons who once sat at the feet of Victor Houteff and believed he was God's chosen

The Little Armageddon

prophet, only to later come to their senses and realize that he was only a misguided soul who truly believed that it was he who would sit on David's throne when the kingdom was established prior to the Loud Cry. Houteff never made that claim in writing, but he did impress that point upon those who were close to him.

One fact becomes very evident from a study of the history of the Shepherd's Rod offshoot, a fact that many of them may not even be aware, and that is that since the movement was launched by Victor Houteff in the 1930s, there have been so many offshoots from the original offshoot that it is impossible to sort out who the "legitimate" representatives of the "Rod" really are. Of course, all of them lay claim to that distinction.

It can be a very frustrating experience to discuss doctrine with Davidians. They are the original spin artists. No matter how clear or how abundant the evidence is that they teach error, they have some comeback that twists and distorts the truth. Very early in my association with them I discerned that modern Davidians share the same defiance of church authority and distrust of church scholars that Victor Houteff possessed. I have found that their membership is mostly composed of former Seventh-day Adventists who felt they were mistreated or otherwise became disgruntled. They are gullible enough to believe that their particular small band of well-intentioned but misguided souls will someday be called upon to gather the masses into what they call the Great Multitude. Meanwhile they continue their mission to subvert the organized work. That, to me, is the height of deception and arrogance.

Seventh-day Adventists and Davidians hold some beliefs in common, but their similarities only run parallel to a point. Beyond that, the two paths diverge off in opposite directions. Davidian teachings of last-day events are totally out of harmony with that time line which God revealed to Ellen White. If you would know end time events, turn to the last few chapters of the book *The Great Controversy*, not to the writings of V. T. Houteff.

While the Seventh-day Adventist Church is busy carrying out their commission to take the gospel to every nation, we must sit by and watch a small handful of isolated groups who call themselves Davidians busy with the task of undermining the faith of church members in their leadership and in the long-established doctrines of the church. While loyal and dedicated Seventh-day Adventists are making determined and successful efforts to preach the three angels messages, Davidians sit on the sidelines and tell us we are going about it all wrong, and that we had better join them before God sends angels to destroy us. In spite of the inability of the several Davidian groups to harmonize on particular points of belief, the one common denominator amongst all of them is that they all believe they are on a mission from God to convert members of the Seventh-day Adventist Church to their particular way of thinking.

Author's Note: Since the mid-1980s I have witnessed once-loyal Seventh-day Adventists get caught up in various Davidian groups, only later to leave the movement and renounce their former Adventist beliefs. I felt a burden to warn my SDA brethren about this formally declared offshoot, and this article is the result. If you have any comments you would like to share about Davidians or this article, please e-mail me at BeaconLightTapes@yahoo.com
Author: *Dwight Turner* **(End of article)**

It is my belief that any church member who reads this article prayerfully and with an open mind will seek to serve the Lord in Spirit and in truth and choose to be on His side in this **Little Armageddon**. Furthermore, I believe they would decide to help to ensure that the Shepherd's Rods do not infiltrate their local church. I also believe that any Shepherd's Rod who reads this article prayerfully and with an honest heart will not remain a Shepherd's Rod. God is an awesomely loving and forgiving God. He will forgive anyone who asks Him. His grace is sufficient.

What a refreshing and redemptive study! May God help us to be faithful Saints!

Praise the Lord!

God's true prophet to the remnant church points men to Jesus Christ and give pointed testimonies that convicted men and encouraged them to order their lives by the will of God[13]. The true prophet of God regards the Bible as the greater light to which her writings, the lesser light points (eg. CM chap. 20, p.126, Ev. Chap. 8, p. 258, SM Chap. 4, p. 31). On the other hand the false prophet (Victor Houteff) sought gain, filthy lucre and desired power for himself, as he sought to persuade others to follow him and embrace his peculiar and erroneous teachings as well as give financial support to him and his cause. The false prophet points to himself and encouraged men to follow him. He asked men to follow and give credence to his ideas. He desired men to follow him and his organization.

What a contrast! False teachings will cause many to end up in destruction – because it destroys the desire for truth (DA Chap. 28, p. 279, etc.). Hence, it is important for us to sit

---
13 Numerous accounts in the Testimonies to the Church and other writings of Ellen G. White.

up, stand up, speak up and take notice of the Shepherd's Rods. To do that we need to pray up, study up and look up to Jesus for help and strength! Jesus said: "…for without me ye can do nothing" (John 15:5, *last part*). Praise the Lord!

The battle of Armageddon involves the conflict between Christ and satan, between God's people and satan's deceived followers. Armageddon is all about worship. God deserves worship and satan wants to be worshipped. Who will we worship in the last days? Where will our allegiance be? The ***Little Armageddon***, which the conflict between the Shepherd's Rod offshoot group and the Church is being called for purpose of this book, is linked to Armageddon. I can almost hear someone asking "How?" It is quite simple: If church members are caught off guard and end up believing the lies taught by the Shepherd's Rod offshoot group they will inevitably end up on the side of satan, for it is satan that originated the false teachings of that group; because satan is behind all lies – for he is the father of lies (John 8:44). It is clear then that this is a very serious matter – because it is a matter of life or death; a matter of eternal destruction or eternal life! Have you begun to get a picture of the seriousness of the conflict?

The devil is the one behind the Shepherd's Rod offshoot group and through the work of this group he hopes to get as much persons as possible to leave the safety of the fold of God[14]. Satan desires to pluck the true worshippers away from the remnant church – the object of his terrible hatred. However, bear in mind that Armageddon is not a battle between equals – it is a battle between the Creator God (Father, Son, and Holy Spirit) and creatures (or created beings, i.e. satan and his demons). So, in this battle God *must* be triumphant! It is *absolutely impossible* for God to

---
14 John 10:27 – 29.

lose! If we enlist on God's side there is absolutely no way satan can overcome us, there's absolutely no way we can lose! It is absolutely impossible for the Creator to be defeated by the created. So, all we need to do is to hold on to Jesus and tell others of Him. We ***will overcome*** "by the blood of the Lamb" and "by the word of" our "testimony".[15]

If you are on the Lord's side, won't you ***stay*** on His side? Dear reader, if you were on His side and strayed into false teachings – won't you please get back on the Lord's side?!

Now is the time to decide – do not delay![16]

Choose ye this day whom you will serve. I, because of the grace of God, choose to serve the Lord (***see*** Joshua 24:15). If we do not choose God now and follow and defend the truth we will not stand at the end. Why would you think that you will choose to worship God then if you won't choose Him now?

A very important aspect of this battle raging in the church is the question of who is a true prophet and who is not. The Lord has provided a prophet for the remnant church. Her name is Ellen Gould White (*nee* Harmon). The prophet is the eye of the church. The prophet gives proper direction to the church and shows the way to progress. If we do not have a true prophet we are in danger of being led astray and being destroyed. If we are to follow the Lord's leading we must hear what His prophet says. It is therefore very important to know who the true prophet is. Since the founder of the Shepherd's Rod group claimed to have the prophetic gift it is important for us to study about this gift. We will look in-depth into this topic in chapter four.

---

15 Revelation 12:11.
16 Hebrews 3:15, 4:7.

Chapter Four

The Importance of the Gift of Prophecy to the Battle of the Little Armageddon

The founder of the Shepherd's Rod, Victor Tasho Houteff, claimed to be a Prophet; but was he? Did he pass the Biblical tests for a Prophet? Read along – and *you decide*.

Before we go on let us recognize that the gift of Prophecy[17] is absolutely crucial to God's end-time Church as the prophecies are the eyes of the Church. After all, the Prophets are regarded as "Seers"[18]. We must be sure who the true Prophet is because it is the teachings of the true Prophet that the people of God must follow. We must ensure we follow the true prophet because our eternal destiny is at stake. It is highly probable that some persons might be duped into following false teachings or false prophecies if they believe that it is coming from a true Prophet of God. Hence, this is not a trivial matter. We need to be fully aware of what the Bible (and the Church) teaches on spiritual gifts if we are to be safe from deception. We need to know and be able

---

17 The Bible and E.G. White's writings.
18 1 Samuel 9:9, 1 Chronicles 9:22; 29:29, Amos 7:12.

to distinguish between the false prophet and the genuine prophet. We need to be knowledgeable on spiritual gifts. This knowledge will assist us in settling in our minds who a true prophet is. Given what we have learnt in the previous chapter, let us now examine what the Church and the Bible teaches on spiritual gifts and the gift of prophecy, so we will be fortified in this respect – and even more ready for battle!

The SDA Church holds the following on Spiritual Gifts:

SPIRITUAL GIFTS

The gifts of the Holy Spirit is mentioned in 1 Cor. 12:28 and Eph. 4:11. As summarized in the latter text they are apostles, prophets, evangelists, pastors, and teachers. They are said to function "for the perfecting of the saints, for the work of the ministry, for the edifying of the body of Christ" (Eph. 4:12).

How many saints have the teachings of the Shepherd's Rods perfected? Perfected in what? And, for what?

On the contrary, the Shepherd's Rods have injured, deceived and confused many saints and caused many others to – eventually – leave the church.

Has the teachings of the Shepherd's Rods been used in or have they led to the work of the Ministry? That is, have they led to the spreading of the gospel (the good news of salvation) to the entire world?

*On the contrary, Shepherd's Rods **do not** participate in witnessing or outreach activities! They instead spend their time luring members out of the church!*

Is the body of Christ (the Church) edified by the teachings of the Shepherd's Rods? In what way(s)? With what?

On the contrary the Shepherd's Rods teach lies and heresies! Much of what they propagate are fictitious!

The list in Corinthians (omitting pastors) adds the following: "miracles, then gifts of healings, helps, governments, diversities of tongues." These gifts were bestowed upon the church at Christ's ascension (Eph. 4:8, 11). They were needed in the early church to confirm the testimony of the early apostles (*see* Heb. 2:4) and to provide guidance and leadership in the young congregations.

In discussing spiritual gifts, ***Seventh-day Adventists have stressed the fact that the Holy Spirit will continue operating in the church until the Second Advent, so that He might be expected to use any of the gifts at any time.*** *(My emphasis)* On the basis of Rev. 12:17 and 19:10 Seventh-day Adventists have held that the gift of prophecy would be manifested in the remnant church (*see* Spirit of Prophecy). *See also* Miracles.

Let us also examine the following:

Prophets, Prophecy and Biblical Tests for a Prophet:

Prophets:

At the dawn of New Testament times the gift of prophecy was revived, with the inspired utterances of Elisabeth (Lk 1:41–45), Simeon, and Anna (ch 2:25–38). A few years later came John the Baptist in the role of Elijah (Lk 1:17). Christ declared John to be a prophet and "more than a prophet" (Mt 11:9, 10). Paul listed the prophetic gift as one of the gifts of the Spirit (1 Cor 12:10), and declared

The Little Armageddon

it to be one of the greatest of these gifts (ch 14:1, 5). As in Old Testament times, the prophetic gift did not necessarily imply the foretelling of future events, though that aspect of prophecy might be included, but consisted chiefly of exhortation and edification (vs 3, 4).

The call to prophetic office, and the accompanying bestowal of the prophetic gift, were acts of God, (*My emphasis*) as in the case of Isaiah (ch 6:8, 9), Jeremiah (ch 1:5), Ezekiel (ch 2:3–5), and Amos (ch 7:15). Moses received his call at the burning bush (Ex 3:1 to 4:17). Elisha's call to the prophetic office was announced by Elijah (1 Ki 19:19, 20; cf. 2 Ki 2:13, 14).

*One has to be both **called** and **gifted** by God to be a prophet. One does not become a prophet through studying and interpreting scripture!*

Accompanying the prophetic call was a special endowment qualifying the prophet to speak for God. (*My emphasis*) This call constituted each prophet a "watchman" over the house of Israel (see Eze. 33:7), and made the prophet strictly accountable to God for faithfully delivering the messages he was commissioned to bear (vv 3, 6).

*One must **be qualified by God** to speak **for God**!*

Having once accepted the prophetic call, a prophet was not free to lay it down at will, as Jeremiah once thought to do (see Jer 20:7–9; 1 Ki 19:9; Jn 1:2–4, 17; 3:2). At times God addressed the prophet in an audible voice (Num 7:89; 1 Sa 3:4), though more commonly in dreams and visions (see Num 12:6; Eze 1:1; Dan 8:2; Mt 1:19). A true prophet (is) **taught by the Spirit of God** (*My emphasis*) (1 Ki 22:24; 2 Chr 15:1; 24:20; Neh 9:30; Eze 11:5; Joel 2:28; Mic 3:8; Zec 7:12; 1 Pe 1:10, 11) and **spoke as he was moved by God's**

Spirit (*My emphasis*) (2 Pe 1:20, 21). **The message he bore was not his own, but God's** (*My emphasis*) (see Eze 2:7; 3:4, 10, 11; cf. Num 22:38; 1 Ki 22:14).

*To **claim** to be a prophet of God when one is not is absolutely terrible; it is tantamount to telling a lie on God!*

If you are teaching under the unction of the Holy Spirit and speaking only as you are moved by Him, **it is impossible for you to speak and teach error!**

In certain instances, as with Nathan (2 Sa 7:3) and Samuel (1 Sa 16:6, 7), a prophet's human judgment was overruled by God. For a time Ezekiel was dumb except when bearing a message from the Lord (see Eze 1:2, 3; 3:26, 27; 33:21, 22). This unique experience was a sign to Ezekiel's hearers that whenever he did speak he did so at God's command. In principle, something similar was true of the other prophets also, for no prophecy of Scripture "came by the impulse of man, but men moved by the Holy Spirit spoke from God" (2 Pe 1:21, RSV). Accordingly, **we "do well to pay attention" to the messages of the prophets** (*My emphasis*) "as to a lamp shining in a dark place, until the day dawns and the morning star rises" in our hearts (2 Pe 1:19, RSV).

*We **must** listen to and **follow** the messages of God's true prophets!*

In some instances the prophets themselves found it necessary to inquire and search diligently into the meaning of the words they had spoken (see 1 Pe 1:10, 11). Daniel, for instance, specifically mentions that he did not understand some portions of the messages entrusted to him (see Dan 8:27; 12:8, 9).

The Little Armageddon

The prophets were distinctly aware of the fact that they spoke for God. Commonly they introduced their messages with such expressions as: "Thus saith the Lord" (Is 66:1), "The word that came to Jeremiah from the Lord" (Jer 11:1), "The vision of Isaiah the son of Amoz" (Is 1:1), "Then I looked, and, behold" (Eze 10:1), "I looked, and, behold" (Rev 4:1), "I saw" (ch 5:1).

God attested the authority of the men whom He called to the prophetic office **by the message they bore** (*My emphasis*) (see 1 Sa 3:19–21), by supernatural signs (2 Ki 2:13–15), by **the fulfillment of their predictions** (*My emphasis*) (Deut 18:22; Jer 28:9), and **by the conformity of their teachings to the will of God as already revealed** (*My emphasis*) (Deut 13:1–3; Is 8:20).

There can be absolutely no room for unfulfilled predictions, absolutely no room for a lack of the Biblical supernatural signs that accompany the prophetic gift and absolutely no room for teachings that are out of harmony with God's already revealed will in the Bible.

Though they were subject to "like passions" as are other human beings, their lives reflected the high principles to which they bore witness (cf. Jas 5:17). ***The SDA Encyclopedia.***

Jesus said that in the last days we must beware of false Christ's and false prophets:

False Prophets:

False prophets often arose, as in the days of Ahab (see 1 Ki 22:6; cf. v 22), Jeremiah (see chs 27:14, 15; 28:1, 2, 5–9, 15–17), Ezekiel (ch 13:17), and Micah (ch 3:11). False prophets could be detected by **their mercenary motives** (ch

3:11), by **their willingness to say what people wished to hear** (Is 30:10; Mic 2:11), **by the failure of their words to come to pass** (Deut 18:22), **by discrepancies between their messages and those of men already attested as prophets** (Deut 13:2, 3; Is 8:20; Jer 27:12–16), by their catering to the wishes of godless people (1 Ki 22:6–8), and **by their own evil lives** (Mt 7:15–20).

In the same way that a prophet is a spokesman, or messenger, for God, so prophecy is any message spoken for God, at His command. It is a special revelation of the divine mind and will, designed to enable man to cooperate intelligently with the infinite purposes of God, and consists essentially in counsel, guidance, reproof, and warning. Since "God does nothing, without revealing his secret to his servants the prophets" (Amos 3:7, RSV), He expects those who read what the prophets have written to give the most diligent heed thereto. In so doing they are certain to "succeed" (2 Chr 20:20, RSV). **Those who fail to heed the words spoken by a prophet as God's messenger or watchman are personally accountable before God** (*My emphasis)* (see Eze 3:17–21; 33:1–9). For the most part, Israel rejected the stirring appeals of the prophets (see Lk 11:47, 48), even as God forewarned Isaiah (Is 6:9–11) and Jeremiah (see Jer 1:8, 17, 19). It was the rejection of the messages of the prophets that brought ruin upon Israel; it led to their refusal to accept their Messiah, and thus to their rejection as a nation. ***SDA Encyclopedia.***

*If **those who teach error** do not heed the counsels and warnings of God through His prophets they will stand alone before God; that will be an absolutely fearsome situation for anyone to be in.*

So, dear reader, was Victor Houteff a Prophet? In the context of the two articles above, I have absolutely no doubt that he most certainly was ... a **FALSE** Prophet (See Chapter Three)

Who then was the genuine modern day Prophet of God? Whose teachings can be followed in addition to those found in the Bible? Let's spend some more time examining the Spirit of Prophecy. This is necessary as an understanding of this matter is pivotal to determining where we should stand in the *Little Armageddon*.

Will you be on God's side or on Satan's side? Read on:

Spirit of Prophecy:

Seventh-day Adventists accept Ellen White's writings as representing the work of the prophetic gift, but not as taking the place of the Bible or as constituting an addition to it. That is the view that she herself maintained: "Brother J would confuse the mind by seeking to make it appear that the light God has given through the Testimonies is an addition to the word of God, but in this he presents the matter in a false light. God has seen fit in this manner to bring the minds of His people to His word to give them a clearer understanding of it" 4T 246).

"The word of God is sufficient to enlighten the most beclouded mind and may be understood by those who have any desire to understand it. . . . To leave men and women without excuse God gives plain and pointed testimonies, bringing them back to the word that they have neglected" (2T 454, 455).

"The written testimonies are not to give new light, but to impress vividly upon the heart the truths of inspiration already revealed" (*ibid.* 605). Ellen White referred to her counsels as "a lesser light to lead men and women to the greater light" (*Review and Herald* 80:15, Jan. 20, 1903).

"The Spirit was not given—nor can it ever be bestowed—to supersede the Bible; for the Scriptures explicitly state that the word of God is the standard by which all teaching and experience must be tested" (GC vii).

*It is truly tragic that **so many are deceived**, being led by **a** spirit!*

In a foreword to volume 1 of Ellen White's *Spiritual Gifts* (1858), Roswell F. Cottrell stated the substance of what has ever since been the denominational position with respect to the gift of prophecy as manifested in Mrs. White. Cottrell recognized the unique position of the Bible as the criterion by which all claims to prophesying must be evaluated. By various texts (Mark 16:15–18; Matt. 28:19, 20; 1 Cor. 12:28; 13:8–13; Eph. 4:11–13; 1 Thess. 5:19–21; Joel 2:28–32; Rev. 12:17; cf. 19:10; 22:9; 1 Cor. 1:4–7) he demonstrated that the Bible itself points to a continuing divine-human channel of communication, and particularly to a renewal of the gifts of the Spirit preceding the promised return of Christ to this earth. Ref. SDA Encyclopedia. Ellen Gould White (nee Harmon)

VISIONS

To Seventh-day Adventists the question of visions has a unique interest because they hold that Ellen G. White received visions from God. In her earlier experience the visions more often occurred during her waking hours, varying in duration from a few minutes to nearly four hours. At such times much was revealed to her. She received her first vision during waking hours in Portland, Maine,

The Little Armageddon

in December 1844 (see 1T 58–61). Her last open vision occurred in a public assembly on the Portland, Oregon, campground in June 1884 (see *General Conference Bulletin* [1893], pp. 19, 20). At the same time, all through this period and continuing on until Mar. 3, 1915 (see *Review and Herald* 92:24, Mar. 25, 1915; 92:3, Apr. 15, 1915; MYP 287), Mrs. White received visions, or prophetic dreams, in the hours of the night.

A number of **Ellen White's visions during waking hours** (*My emphasis*) were accompanied by **physical phenomena** (*My emphasis*), numerous eyewitness accounts of which have been widely published. The first indication of the vision was usually an animated exclamation of "Glory!" or "Glory to God!" often repeated two or three times. At this juncture Mrs. White **lost all consciousness of her surroundings**. (*My emphasis*) While president of the General Conference of Seventh-day Adventists, George I. Butler, in 1874, gave a contemporary eyewitness account of such visions: "They generally, but not always, occur in the midst of earnest seasons of religious interest while the Spirit of God is specially present. . . . The time Mrs. White is in this condition has varied from fifteen minutes to one hundred and eighty. During this time **the heart and pulse continue to beat**, the **eyes are always wide open**, (*My emphasis*) and seem to be gazing at some far-distant object, and are never fixed on any person or thing in the room. They **are always directed upward**. (*My emphasis*) They exhibit a pleasant expression. . .

"While she is in vision, **her breathing entirely ceases**. (*My emphasis*) No breath ever escapes her nostrils or lips when in this condition. This has been proved by many witnesses, among them physicians of skill, and themselves unbelievers in the visions, on some occasions being appointed by a public congregation for the purpose. . . . When she goes into this condition, there is no appearance of swooning or faintness, her face retains its natural color, and the blood circulates as usual. **Often she loses her strength temporarily** (*My emphasis)* and reclines or sits; but at other times she stands up. She moves her arms gracefully, and often her face is lighted up with radiance as though the glory of Heaven rested upon her. She is utterly unconscious of every thing going on around her, while she is in vision, having no knowledge whatever of what is said and done in her presence. . . .

"Calm, dignified, and impressive, her very appearance strikes the beholder with reverence and solemnity. There is nothing fanatical in her appearance. When she comes out of this condition she speaks and writes from time to time what she had seen while in vision, . . . for **many things have thus been related which it was impossible for her to know in any other way**" (*My emphasis*) (*Review and Herald* 43:201, June 9, 1874).

Similar in many respects to the prophet Daniel (See Daniel Chapters 10 & 5)

On several occasions, while in vision, Ellen White lifted and held a large family Bible on the outstretched hand for extended periods of time, at least on two occasions repeating various verses from it. One weighing 18 pounds she held for nearly a half hour. This has been testified to by many and competent witnesses. **Neither Ellen White nor those around her could induce, prevent, or interfere with a vision**. (*My emphasis)* These experiences never left her worn or spent; on the contrary they refreshed her. There were times when she experienced physical healing in connection with a vision. In 1868 James White reported that, between

The Little Armageddon

1844 and that time, Mrs. White had had between 100 and 200 such visions.

Seventh-day Adventists do not cite any physical manifestations as unanswerable proof that God gave visions to Ellen White. The supernatural physical manifestations that accompanied the visions appear to have been simply a means of engendering confidence; they were secondary, not primary, proof (My emphasis). They occurred mostly in her earlier years before it was possible to judge her experience by the fruits of her lifework (cf. Matt. 7:15, 16, 20). SDA's can now see the results in the richness of her personal religious experience, in the elevated spiritual experience of men and women who accept and follow her counsels, and in the progress of the church as it followed her counsels.

In the experience of Ellen White, ***visions in the night were much more frequent than the visions accompanied by the physical phenomena*** (*My emphasis*) and were usually less comprehensive in content and scope. All through her life experience it was not uncommon for her to have visions while she was praying (TM 461), or even while she was writing or engaged in public address.

Often it seemed that the information imparted to her was gained through the ordinary organs of sense, such as seeing and hearing. In her introduction to The Great Controversy she refers to "the scenes of the past and the future" that passed before her, and tells of being "permitted to behold the working, in different ages, of the great controversy" (pp. xi, x).

On this point Ellen White's experience was like that of the biblical prophets. "In the case of visions the scenery passed before their mind, something like a panoramic view of a landscape, gradually unfolding, in symbolical imagery, forms of glory or of gloom; accompanied with actions of a corresponding character, not unfrequently (sic) exhibiting, as in actual occurrence, the future and distant events" (Cyclopaedia of Biblical, Theological, and Ecclesiastical Literature, vol. 8, p. 648).

The impressions made upon her mind were deep and lasting, enabling her to recognize months or years later a voice previously heard in vision or to identify persons seen in the vision. Ellen White wrote in 1860: "As inquiries are frequently made as to my state in vision, and after I come out, I would say that when the Lord sees fit to give a vision, I am taken into the presence of Jesus and the angels, and am entirely lost to earthly things. I can see no farther than the angel directs me. My attention is often directed to scenes transpiring upon earth.

"At times I am carried far ahead into the future and shown what is to take place. Then again I am shown things as they have occurred in the past. "After I come out of vision I do not at once remember all that I have seen, and the matter is not so clear before me until I write, then the scene rises before me as was presented in vision, and I can write with freedom. Sometimes the things which I have seen are hid from me after I come out of vision, and I cannot call them to mind until I am brought before a company where that vision applies, then the things which I have seen come to my mind with force. **I am just as dependent upon the Spirit of the Lord in relating or writing a vision, as in having the vision**. (*My emphasis*) It is impossible for me to call up things which have been shown me unless the Lord brings them before me at the time that He is pleased to have me relate or write them" (2SG 292, 293).

Some years later Ellen White remarked: "Although I am as dependent upon the Spirit of the Lord in writing my views as I am in receiving them, yet the words I employ in describing what I have seen are my own" (*Review and Herald* 30:260, Oct. 8, 1867).

Source: TAGnet Search: Biblical Tests of a Prophet and Daniel Prophecy Study # 25: The Gift of Prophecy.

The true prophetess said:

"I have all faith in God. I know the perfection of His government. He works at my right hand and at my left. While I am writing out important matter, He is beside me, helping me. He lays out my work before me, and when I am puzzled for a fit word with which to express my thought, He brings it clearly and distinctly to my mind. I feel that every time I ask, even while I am still speaking, He responds, 'Here am I'" (letter 127, 1902). **SDA Encyclopedia.**

Did anything like what was described above as happening to Ellen White happen to Victor Houteff?

Did he *claim* that any such thing happened to him? Were there any witnesses - *if* any such thing happened?

For me, the simple, one word answers is "*No*".

So, in the *Little Armageddon* whose side should we be on? What should be the foundation on which we stand?

Did Victor Houteff satisfy the Biblical Tests of a prophet?

He most certainly did not. For one thing, much of what he taught was contrary to what God had already revealed on the subject.

The true Prophet of God, when writing expressly for God, ***must be correct one hundred percent of the time***.

I believe the foregoing, to this point, has settled this question ... without - the - shadow - of - a – doubt!

Let us therefore ponder two very crucial questions at this time:

Q. If Victor Houteff was not a true Prophet, what was he?

A. A FALSE PROPHET.

Q. If Houteff was not a true Prophet what does that make ***his followers***?

You, dear reader, should be in a position now to posit an answer to that question!

Now that we have dispensed with Victor Houteff and his claim, let us look at the following chapter to ascertain more on the Biblical tests of a prophet. Let us plunge into some *more study*.

Grab the Sword of the Spirit and let's go!

Chapter Five

Biblical Tests for a Prophet (A Study):

The following study is a bonus and will help to fortify us and also deepen our knowledge on the tests of a prophet. I hope it will benefit you at least as much as it did me.

We highly recommend that you breathe a prayer to the Holy Spirit - the Spirit of truth who will teach you all things - for wisdom and understanding **before you read this study.**

DANIEL PROPHECY STUDY # 25[19]

THE GIFT OF PROPHECY

Ever since the fall of humanity, God has communicated to us through the prophets. Daniel stands in direct line with the many other great prophets of Scripture. The visions and dreams that he saw and recorded in his book are part of the collection of the writings of the prophets. How thankful we are for this tremendous revelation that God has given to us in the Bible. We are surely indebted to the prophets for the messages they have sent.

---

[19] Taken from the Internet from a free website that is available for online study. Source: http://anotherviewpoint.netadvent.org/Daniel/25.htm Web page maintained by Allen Roy.

In this lesson lets examine the gift of prophecy as it appears in the life of the prophet Daniel and in the rest of the Bible, and then see if the gift of prophecy is still around today.

THE PROPHET DANIEL

1. **How does God communicate to a prophet? (Numbers 1:26)** When a prophet of the LORD is among you,
   I reveal myself to him in ___
   I speak to him in ___

   NOTE: A dream occurs while the prophet sleeps. A vision occurs while he is awake. These do not arise out of ordinary experiences of life, but are inspired by the Holy Spirit. **Did Daniel have dreams and visions? (Daniel 7:1; 8:1) Describe some of the physical phenomena that accompanied Daniel while in vision. (Dan.10: 8, 9, 10, 17, 18)**

   a. I had no ___ left
   b. I fell into a deep___, my face to the ground.
   c. A hand ___ me and set me trembling on my hands and knees.
   d. My ___ is gone.
   e. he ___ me.

   NOTE: Certain physical phenomena accompany the prophets while in vision, demonstrating to those around them that they are receiving something that came from a supernatural source.

THE GIFT OF PROPHECY IN BIBLE TIMES

2. **Who is the source of the messages that the prophets received in vision? (2 Peter 1:21)**

   But men spoke from God as they were ___ along by the ___

3. **Will God do anything on the earth without first telling His prophets? (Amos 3:7)**

   Surely the Sovereign Lord does ___ without revealing his ___ to his servants the ___.

   NOTE: Before God does anything of significance involving His people on the earth, He first of all reveals it to the prophets through dreams and visions. Throughout Biblical history, God spoke through a variety of individuals. Daniel was not unique in receiving the prophetic gift. God chose women too, such as Miriam (Exo.15:20), Huldah (2 Chron. 34:22) and Anna (Luke 2:36). God chose to give the prophetic gift to those individuals who could best serve Him at the time.

   As one examines the prophetic gift in Scripture, it becomes clear that there were two basic groups of prophets:

   a. Those whose written revelations are recorded in the Bible, such as Moses, Daniel, and John the Revelator;

   b. Those whose writings did not form part of sacred Scripture or who only gave oral presentations, such as Enoch, Elijah, and John the Baptist, and yet these prophets were just as inspired as the other Bible prophets.

   Thus people can be regarded as prophets and not have their writings regarded as a part of sacred Scripture.

- **What is one of the gifts that God has given to His New Testament church? (Eph.4: 11)**

    Who gave some to be apostles, some to be___, some to be evangelists, and some to be pastors and teachers...

    NOTE: The gift to be a prophet is one of the spiritual gifts that God has given the New Testament church. Do we still have evangelists, pastors, and teachers today? Then why not prophets?

- **How long were these gifts, including the gift of being a prophet, to remain in the church? (Eph.4: 13)**

    Until we all reach ___ in the faith and in the ___ of the Son of God and become___, attaining to the whole measure of the ___ of Christ.

    NOTE: This text makes it very clear that these spiritual gifts, including the gift of prophecy, are to remain in the church until the church reaches perfection, which will not be until the second coming of Jesus. Paul's point is very clear: as long as we are on this earth we will need all the gifts of the Spirit, including the gift of prophecy.

- **What is the purpose of the gift of Prophecy? (1 Cor.14: 3)** ___, encouragement, and ___.

    NOTE: The gift of prophecy is not primarily the ability to predict the future. Some Bible prophets, such as Daniel, did predict the future, but many others did not. Their work was to strengthen, encourage, and comfort the church. Thus one can be a prophet without necessarily predicting the future.

THE GIFT OF PROPHECY BEYOND BIBLE TIMES

- **What counsel did the apostle Paul give the Thessalonians concerning the gift of prophecy? (1 Thess.5:19 – 21)** Do not treat prophecies with

The Little Armageddon

___ ___ everything.
Hold ___ to the good.

NOTE: If God did not plan to send prophets after Bible times, Paul would have cautioned the Thessalonians to disregard anyone in the future who could claim to have the prophetic gift. Instead, Paul tells them not to treat them with contempt, but to test them, and if they prove true, to hold on to their teachings.

- What kind of prophets did Jesus warn against? (Matt.7:15) ___ prophets.

NOTE: If there were not going to be any genuine prophets, Jesus would have warned against all prophets. The fact that He warned against false prophets indicates the presence of the genuine.

- **Who does Malachi suggest will appear before the coming of the Lord? (Mal. 4:5)**

I will send you the prophet ___ before that great and dreadful day of the LORD comes.

NOTE: Connected with the coming of Elijah is the gift of prophecy. It is not simply Elijah, but Elijah the prophet who is to come before the coming of the great and dreadful day of the Lord.

- **What great revival of the prophetic gift did the prophet Joel foresee? (Joel 2:28)**
Your sons and daughters will ___
Your old men will dream ___
Your young men will see ___

- **At what time will this great prophetic outpouring take place? (Joel 2:31)**

    The sun will be turned into___ .... before the coming of the ___ and ___ day of the LORD.

    NOTE: Joel predicted that sometime after the darkening of the sun, which was fulfilled on May 19, 1780, and before the coming of the Lord, this great prophetic gift would be restored to the church.

- **In what group of people would the prophetic gift appears at this time? (Joel 2:28-32)**

    Among the ___ whom the LORD calls.

    NOTE: The survivors are the last of God people in the last days -- the remnant.

- **What are two key Bible identification points of the remnant? Rev.12:17**

    a. Those who obey God's ___ And hold to the ___ of Jesus.

    NOTE: Joel predicted that the remnant church would have the gift of prophecy. One of the identifying marks of the remnant church, according to Revelation 12:17 is that they not only keep the commandments of God, but they also hold to the testimony of Jesus.

- **What is the testimony of Jesus? Rev.19: 10**
    The testimony of Jesus is the spirit of ___.

- **Is the spirit of prophecy and prophets the same**

thing? Compare Rev.19: 10; and 22:8, 9.

I am a fellow servant with you and your brothers who hold to the testimony of Jesus... 19:10
I am a fellow servant with you and your brothers the ___ 22:9

NOTE: Revelation 19:10 and 22:9 are identical, except that Revelation 19:10 refers to the spirit of prophecy and Revelation 22:9 calls them prophets. Thus one of the marks that identifies the remnant church is that they will have the gift of prophecy.

THE GIFT OF PROPHECY TODAY

The Bible foretells that in the last days before the coming of the Lord, God will raise up a remnant, a church that will keep all the commandments of God, and that will also have the gift of prophecy. In order to qualify as the remnant church, the church must have the gift of prophecy. It is one of the special marks of identification of the last-day church. The same gift that inspired the prophet Daniel will be duplicated in the end time by a restoration of the gift of prophecy to the church. Did God fulfill this prediction? Did He send the gift of prophecy to the remnant church after` the darkening of the sun in 1780?

In December of 1844, a 17-year-old girl named Ellen Harmon, in frail health, possessing only a third-grade education, received a vision while kneeling in prayer with a group of young women in Portland, Maine. She shrank from the prospect of being a prophet, yet she wished to be obedient to the heavenly vision, and so she related what God had shown her. For 69 years she continued to receive visions and dreams from the Lord. Ellen (Harmon) White became one of the most prolific female writers in history. Many of her books are still in publication today. Was this a genuine or counterfeit manifestation? Was it a fulfillment of the Biblical promise that the prophetic gift would be restored to the church at the end time?

- **What physical phenomena accompanied Ellen's visions?**

Ellen White's experience was very similar to that of the prophet Daniel (see question 3).

a. She did not breath during many visions. Sometimes her visions lasted for as long as four hours. Physicians who examined her in vision marveled that she did not breathe, yet still lived.

b. At times, like Daniel, she experienced a loss of physical strength, which was then replaced by supernatural strength. During one vision she held a seventeen-pound family Bible outstretched in her hand for thirty minutes. At that time she weighed 97 pounds and was in frail health. Obviously here was supernatural strength.

The physical phenomena accompanying the prophets indicate that there is something supernatural about their experience; however, the physical phenomena don't tell us whether

The Little Armageddon

the experience is from God or Satan. We must examine the Biblical tests of a prophet to determine whether the prophet is from God or Satan.

- **What is the first Biblical test of a prophet? Isa.8: 20**

To the ___ and to the ___.

> **NOTE:** The expression "the law and the testimony" is an Old Testament expression for the Bible. "The Law" referred to the first five books of Moses, and "the testimony" referred to the testimony of the prophets and the rest of the Old Testament. The basic meaning of the text is that the prophet must agree with Scripture, or he is not a genuine prophet. This point must be very clear. Any person today who claims to be a prophet must be tested by Scripture. What God reveals to His prophets today will not disagree with what he has previously revealed in the Bible. **The Bible is the supreme revelation. If a prophet disagrees with Scripture, that person is a false prophet** (Author's emphasis). You are invited to take any book written by Ellen and examine what she says with what the Bible says. You will find that Ellen agrees with the Bible.

- **What is the second test of a prophet? 1 John 4:2**

Every spirit that acknowledges that ___ has come in the ___ is from God.

> **NOTE:** True prophets will attest to the humanity

and divinity of Jesus. They will elevate and exalt Jesus Christ. To test Ellen in this area, one has only to read her books such as Steps to Christ, DOA, COL or Thoughts from the Mount of Blessing and one very quickly sees that she beautifully fulfills this test of a prophet. Another example of Ellen's constant uplifting of Jesus is seen in the passage that gives counsel to pastors on how they should preach.

- **What is the third Bible test of a prophet? Matt.7: 20**

By their ___ you will recognize them.

NOTE: The Bible prophets were not perfect, nor is any prophet perfect; they were human. But the general tendency of the life must be in harmony with the Word of God.

- **What is the fourth Bible test of a prophet? Jer. 28:9**

But the prophet....will be recognized as one truly sent by the Lord ___ if his prediction comes ___.

NOTE: The final Biblical test of the prophet is fulfilled predictions. Bible prophets gave predictions that dealt with main themes of the great controversy and salvation, not mundane things such as winning elections, astrology, etc. If the prophet predicts the future, it will come to pass. If the prophecy fails, the prophet would not be genuine. Like most Bible prophets, Ellen did not give a lot of predictions. Her work was to strengthen, encourage, and comfort the church. Yet there were times when she did give predictions, and on these she can be tested. Like Bible prophets, her predictions were sometimes conditional upon obedience, but her insights clearly reveal the prophetic voice speaking through her.

As one examines the life and ministry of Ellen White in relationship to four Bible tests of a prophet, it becomes very clear that **she meets every one of the tests** (Author's emphasis). The physical phenomena indicated that we are dealing with a supernatural force from the Lord.

- **What is the relationship of Ellen to the Bible?**

    She ___ the Bible.

NOTE: Perhaps the most important point of Ellen's ministry is the fact that she consistently pointed people to the Bible. She always uplifted the Bible. The Bible predicted this gift would come in the last days to be a tremendous blessing to the church. The evidence points out that it has come.

Our God is such an awesome God! God is so loving and kind, merciful and longsuffering towards us. God desires all men to be saved (1 Tim. 2:3, 4). On the other hand, satan wants all men to be lost. God is preparing a complete end to satan and his demons (Matt. 25:41). The total destruction that will occur in hellfire is not intended by God for humankind. However, since God is love He allows man to choose for himself. Sadly, most of the human race will be totally destroyed in hellfire with the devil and his angels because *they chose* to follow a way other than the way of Jesus who is the only way (John 14:6, Acts 4:12). There can only be *one* way, there can be only *one* truth. The devil does not want anyone to know the truth because he knows that following truth will ultimately result in the salvation of mankind (John 14:6, John 17:17, John 8:32). Dear reader, we need to wake up and realize that we must stand for truth even though the heavens fall (Education, p. 57). We also must decidedly reject falsehood whenever and wherever it rears its despicable head! We must seek to eradicate it from our individual lives, from our families, from the church, from our learning institutions, from the communities in which we live; as best as we possibly can… by the grace of God. While the *Little Armageddon* rages we cannot be complacent, nor can we be indifferent; we cannot remain neutral nor fear to stand on the side of right because of regard for what others might say (see Daniel 3:12). We must <u>*choose*</u> to be on the Lord's side. We must consciously and determinedly choose to be on God's side and to *totally reject* false teachings and those persons that perpetrate same. It has been said that for evil to triumph all it takes is for good men (good people; saints of God) to remain silent (when they should both speak out and take action against false teachings). Finally, if there is anyone that is lost because of following falsehood it cannot be God's fault. Every one of us must give an account of ourselves; if we are lost we have no one else to blame but ourselves (Romans 14:11, 12). God has made all the provisions for our salvation – we must grasp that salvation and hold on to it for dear life; we cannot afford to let go – we cannot afford to abandon truth (*consider* Phil. 2:12, 13; 1 Cor. 10:12, 13, John 16:13, Eph. 4:15, 1 John 1:6,7; 2 John 1:9-11).

With all of this we are still not fully ready for the battle…

The Little Armageddon

Sharing something with someone is often a way to identify with the person or, to help the person. The experiences we have can be extremely valuable in helping us to make right decisions as we seek to be victorious in our Christian experience and become perfect as our Father in heaven is perfect.

Militarily, know–how and experience is vital in determining whether or not a battle is won. We have all heard the saying: "knowledge is power". Of course, sometimes we will need to consult with others; sometimes we need to get some help – some real good advice from someone who knows and has a wealth of experience. It could mean the difference between life and death.

Proverbs 27:17

Chapter Six

Preparing for the Enemy by Identifying the Enemy

Before we even identify them, dear reader, here are some *ammunition* that you can keep handy for the battle of the *Little Armageddon*. The battle at times can be fierce, fast and furious … and there might be no time for long studies and explanations, no time for negotiation … and there is definitely *no room for compromise.* If the entire Bible is the Sword of the Spirit the following texts might be regarded as some darts to keep handy to throw at the devil, his demons and human representatives; aim for the *eyes*!

Here are a Few Bible References on False Prophets and False Teachers:

1. Acts 20: 26 – 32 ("…feed the Church of God…")
2. John 10:9 – 15 ("…the good shepherd giveth his life for the sheep…")
3. Matthew 24:24 – 26 ("…there shall arise false Christs and false prophets")
4. 1 Timothy 4:1, 2 ("…in the latter times some shall depart from the faith…")

The Little Armageddon

5. 2 Timothy 4:1 – 5 ("…they shall turn away their ears from the truth…")
6. Isaiah 8:20 ("To the law and to the testimony…")
7. Jeremiah 28:15 – 17 ("…thou makest this people to trust in a lie.")
8. 2 John 1:9 – 11 ("..receive him not into your house…")
9. 1 John 4:1 ("…many false prophets are gone out into the world.")
10. Matthew 7:15 – 24 ("Beware of false prophets…")
11. 1 John 2:18, 19 ("They went out from us…")
12. 1 John 1:6, 7 ("But if we walk in the light…")
13. 2 Peter 2:1 – 3 ("…who privily shall bring in damnable heresies, …")

Please, get to know at least some of these references and commit portions of them to memory as much as possible – you can do it! (Phil. 4:13) Now, to the task:

Now that the false nature of the Shepherd's Rod group has been *clearly shown*, you might be asking: How can I identify the persons that belong to this group? Could I have been talking to one such person for years and did not know?

There is no easy answer and no one identifying mark per se, that is conclusive in terms of identifying a member of the group. However, the following list should at least help you to answer your questions:

John Churchill

The Lay Minister Says:
How to Identify Shepherd's Rods

1. Look for a combination of things: The females, young or old, usually wear hats to church and dress very conservatively / traditionally (full dresses, long dresses / long skirts), many times the females will wear black and white outfits (usually black skirts, white blouses) and often carry handbags to church; and the males carry large bags or attaché cases (usually used to carry the Shepherd's Rod books written by V. T. Houteff),
2. They usually refuse to pray without first kneeling, i.e., for example, they usually kneel for prayer even when everyone else is standing AND they usually will either stay seated or kneel when the congregation is asked to stand for prayer,
3. They usually have a general appearance of humility / claim to humility / is usually attacking others accusing them of not being humble / accusing others that they do not have the Spirit of God (as a result),
4. They usually claim to be the bearers of "higher light", "better light" or "new light" (i.e. they claim to have some better teaching or enlightened understanding of the beliefs of the church and the scriptures),
5. Some are brave enough to invite you to have further studies with them – on the sermon preached in church that day/night, or, on some other topic (the 144,000 is a favorite topic for them),
6. They tend to be very stubborn and usually stick to their views even in the light of plain scripture that proves they are wrong,

The Little Armageddon

7. They are often disgruntled with church leaders or church leadership on a whole and are often disrespectful of church leaders and the Conference or, are very critical of the Conference (Usually, accusing the Church Organization of misuse of tithe; corruption; etc.),
8. Handing out or having in their possession leaflets / books / literature that contain spurious or false teachings (especially with the intent to persuade others to believe and accept the teachings they contain),
9. They sometimes sit in groups but at other times will scatter, especially when in a large church or in very large crowds (for example, at Church Conventions, et cetera); so, usually, if you see one, there are likely to be others around,
10. They are usually very offended or incensed when they are told that they are *not* Seventh-day Adventists,
11. They are equally upset when they are told that they are teachers of falsehood,
12. They are usually either misquoting or misinterpreting scripture [Dear reader, if you are not acquainted with the Word of God you won't know if / when they are doing this – study the word! (2 Tim. 2:15)],
13. They are usually misquoting, quoting out of context or otherwise misinterpreting the writings of Ellen G. White – *to suit their arguments* [Dear reader, if you are not very acquainted with the Spirit of Prophecy writings you would not be able to recognize this – please, start reading them now if you are not already doing so!].

Remember, dear Reader, we are in a **Great Controversy** ... and the devil is waging a serious war within the Seventh-day Adventist Movement. The devil was one of the covering Cherubs in Heaven; he was right next to the throne of God! He started in Heaven, sowing discord amongst the angels – and he succeeded in getting one third of them on his side! (Rev. 12:4) Do you think that he is an enemy we can play with? He will devour us – if we *once* step outside of God's protection (1 Peter 5:8).

Many Leaders in the Church are smiling and shaking hands for peace with an enemy that intends to plunge a dagger in their heart! This enemy will use every means and any means possible to steal from us (our joy, our confidence, our zeal, our values, our doctrines, etc.), kill us and destroy us through his deceptions... if at all possible (John 10:9, 10; Matthew 24:24). But, thank God, greater is He that is within us than he that is in the world! (1 John 4:4).

This battle that is going on within the Church is just the *Little Armageddon* - as the forces of evil have arrayed themselves against the Sons of God (John 1:12). This is serious! Dear Reader, in any war there is strategy employed ... and satan sure has some strategies in this offshoot group. What are some strategies used by the Shepherd's Rods? Brace yourself! Or get down into a foxhole! The following might shock you or hammer you into the ground - or even blow you away:

Strategies of the Shepherd's Rod Offshoot Group

1. They have been known to invite church members to lunch with the aim of getting them away from the company of other members – so they can introduce their peculiar brand of teaching in a way that is overwhelming,

The Little Armageddon

2. They will also accept lunch invitations from unsuspecting members / members whom they think are weak – to seek an opportunity to introduce their false doctrines,
3. They *pretend* to be Seventh-day Adventists,
4. They often have secret meetings (usually, changing the venue periodically) to which they invite members of the Church (usually those that show an interest to study with them),
5. They make frequent references to Ellen G. White's writings (***to try to justify*** their false teaching),
6. They present themselves as having a superior understanding of the Word of God (and the Spirit of Prophecy) and tell people that this is because they are privy to "new light" or "higher light" or "better light",
7. They will not (or usually do not) take counsel from church Leaders (their pride wont allow them; remember, they believe they have "higher light" or superior knowledge or inspiration),
8. They will often whisper to church members in church, while service is going on, with the aim of obtaining sympathy for the group and / or, are usually busy criticizing while a sermon or some other way of revelation of the Word is going on – of course, pushing their own views or agenda,
9. They will sometimes disrupt Sabbath School when the lesson review is going on OR try to take over the lesson review OR totally dominate the discussion – of course, with *their ideas* about the study (especially if the topic is one on which they generally believe differently or, any related subject. They seem to have a particular liking for the topic of the 144,000!),

10. Their special (or favorite) targets are the **newly converted members**! They will even attend baptisms – where they literally choose those they will target after the baptism! They observe members keenly to try to find out if they are not yet *steeped in the Word of God* (For example, if they observe a new member struggling to move from text to text during a sermon or other presentation they may target them; they will also listen for the types of questions that an individual member or new convert may ask, etc.); in other words, they target members that they assess to be "weak" or, not yet fully acquainted with the Word of God (A typical tactic that is even employed in the animal kingdom! *Grab the weak ones!*)
11. They also target members that are upset with the Church in general OR with the Leadership of the particular Local Church OR the Conference OR the wider church organization OR even the member that is upset with another member or feel they were wronged in some way,
12. They will resort to ***outright lying*** in order to conceal their personal identity or church of origin (OR, they will sometimes say where they are from in a non-specific way; for example, telling the area or town but not the specific church),
13. They will also resort to outright lying in order to conceal their real mission (which is really to deceive and separate the flock and draw away disciples after themselves – I have absolutely no doubt about that!),
14. They are usually steeped in the study of the Word of God and the Spirit of Prophecy writings (sadly, today ***many Seventh-day Adventist Christians***

The Little Armageddon

are not studying their Bibles and many do not read or care about Ellen G. White's inspired writings; they are also not getting to know Jesus more each day – this makes them choice candidates for attacks from the Shepherd's Rods!),

15. More often than not they have a copy (or copies) of Victor Houteff's writings / books / pamphlets / tracts with them – which they study in-depth and take pride in knowing their teachings. In other words, they are usually prepared – with their tools and weapons ready! That usually explains the bags and attaché cases they carry around. Sadly, that's more than what many Seventh-day Adventists are today – prepared! Some members refuse to even take a Bible with them to church!

16. The Rods sometimes leave their literature on seats, moving from seat to seat, thereby distributing them throughout the church [this often goes unnoticed by the non -vigilant, the unaware OR the totally ignorant member or Leader of the Church! (OR, whatever gathering they are at).

17. The Rods sometimes turn up in droves at large Church Conventions, Lay Preachers' Institutes, and even at Local Churches. Briefly, some of them are real brazen!

18. There are some Rods who are brazen enough to just take **the direct approach** and just hand out their literature to members / whoever will receive it. If more Seventh-day Adventists were even half as brazen as some of these offshoots today – the Church would have torn down the kingdom of satan and fulfill Jesus' great commission already! The truth is, some Seventh-day Adventists are afraid and ashamed to defend what they believe; a

very sad state of affairs.

<u>Note Well:</u>
They usually (if / when they can) observe those who pick up the literature and then do follow-up work – offering to explain the literature or to study with the curious readers about the subject in the literature. What a strategy!?

19. The Rods have been known to offer financial or other assistance to individuals as a means of winning their confidence or getting them to come over on their side [This is a rather dated strategy of people who teach falsehood; many are willing to pay to get persons into their church or group; this was encountered by Ellen White during her work in Italy. See: Historical Sketches of the Foreign Missions of the Seventh-day Adventists (1886), p. 244].

Framework / Summary of Their Strategy
The Shepherd's Rod offshoot group / its members seem to have a particular strategy that they follow in doing their work, as follows:

1. Scouting:
They will check out the church, that is, they will attend the church and observe the members and leadership, participate in discussions (like Sabbath School lesson discussion), see how alert or aware the general membership and leaders are, et cetera. In other words, they try to find out as much as possible about the church and its membership.

2. Profiling Members:
Having scouted out the church the Rod now has enough information and can do an actual assessment of the situation and start putting the members into categories. They then determine which members are - in their estimation - more firm or serious in their walk with God or determine those who are so called weak members.

3. Targeting Members:
Having scouted and decided on which members to approach they then begin to encounter specific members, engaging them in flattering conversation and giving them materials to study (literature, audio / video tapes, CD's, DVD's, et cetera).

As Seventh-day Adventists might we learn from any of these strategies? Does being aware of these strategies strengthen us in our fight? Knowing an enemy's game-plan makes it easier for us to fight and fight intelligently! In other words, *to be forewarned is to be forearmed* and, at least in this case, **knowledge is indeed power.** Let us ask for grace to overcome! Let us study the truth! God's Word is truth and it is that truth that will sanctify us! (John 17:17). Praise the Lord!

Having been prepared is good. However, sometimes a well prepared, fully equipped soldier *literally freezes* when faced with the enemy and the actual war. How do we confront the enemy? That's what the following chapter is about. Please read on.

Chapter Seven

Confronting False Teachers

And so now we will move on to the brass tacks! To where ***the rubber meets the road***. Let's look at a real case ... a battle, no less. Let us take all the lessons we can from it.

Another Battle:

Confronting False Teachers: A Prescription for Action - a Surgical Operation (Nipping it in the Bud!)

The Problem:

A set of Shepherd's Rods (or Davidian Seventh-day Adventists) persisting in their attendance at a Local Seventh-day Adventist Church and starting to take action towards members and putting forward their false doctrines (by making negative comments to members while the Sabbath School lesson is going on and, engaging members in conversation after the Divine Service and stating who they are, etc. - ready for battle). Their background: mainly one family (about four or five members) plus one member from a nearby church (a former new convert that, unfortunately, joined the group). The family was formerly members of another church in another District of Churches within the Local Conference.

The Little Armageddon

The First Elder at the nearby Church had called and cautioned the First Elder at the church presently under attack, giving a full description of the group and what to expect ... and also informing that one of the new members of his church was "taken away" by the group (this is war!) ... and that this member now refuses to even talk to the Leaders of the Church. Letter(s) had since been given to the group asking them to stop visiting that church. This was done ***after*** other redemptive actions were taken (including the intervention of one Pastor who spent several hours in discussions with the group)... and those efforts had all failed.

Steps taken at the church under attack:

(a) The ***Elder*** of the ***church informed the members of the presence of the group***: The church was told what the most likely intention and mission of the group was and the dangers that the teachings of this group posed to the Church; the Church was therefore cautioned and put on *full alert.* Scripture passages were used to show the warnings of Jesus and the Apostles (Peter and Paul) concerning false teachers.

(b) The Elder *confronted* and spoke to the Shepherd's Rod on their second visit to the church to ascertain from them what their mission was:

Their reaction:
They were "represented" by the leader (the mother of the family) and also by their recent convert. Their reaction was one of resentment, and, they felt offended that they were being questioned. In summary, they felt they had a right to come to the church and a right to talk to members about their contrary beliefs - as they wished. They challenged the authority of the Elder of the church to question them; they resented the Elder's confronting and questioning them as to

their reason for being at the church as they felt he had no right to do so! The Elder was asked: "Are you a police?" and, "Why are you questioning us?"[20]

The Elder then told them clearly and specifically not to seek to proselytize anyone at the church. They were welcomed however, **if** they were there just to sit quietly and worship. On that occasion they were (again) allowed to stay at the Church.

(c) At the second visit in question the situation was also addressed through ***a redemptive message*** during a Divine Service: Members were educated about the group that is attacking the church, their real mission, their strategies, how to recognize them, what not to do with regards to them, what can ultimately happen if the group is allowed to have "free reign" in the church, etc. The special redemptive aspect of the message was to not only appeal to the brethren to exercise caution, study God's words and have good reasons for their faith to be able to stand up to false teachers in these times, but to issue an appeal to the Davidians / Shepherd Rods themselves to come back on the **true platform** of the true teachings of God's Church before it's too late!

Other Steps taken:

1. Information was disseminated to a few members in the form of the written text of the sermon that was presented (which included some research on the movement, several scriptures on false teachers and false prophets, etc., etc.). A copy of the sermon had been requested by several members after the said presentation.

2. The Shepherd's Rods were asked to leave the Church and not return, given their persistence in attending and apparent

---

[20] This was asked by the new recruit!

The Little Armageddon

5) Imagine someone coming to your home to **steal your children** or, to tell them things that **confuse them** and teach them **things that are contrary to what you have been telling them and how you have been training them** (i.e. in the right way, the way of the Lord) and causing them to start to question *your authority* and not liking *you* anymore? And wanting to leave the home? Would you tolerate that? What would you do? Should the church family be any different?

6) Church leaders have a great responsibility in this matter:
While every member of the church has some amount of responsibility in the matter, **the leaders are fully accountable** before God to be good Under-shepherds of His Flock (this is <u>God's</u> Church!). The leader in God's church <u>cannot</u> afford to be like a hireling – they must truly love, care for and protect the sheep; leaders **must** stand up and deal with these situations as best as they possibly can; and, more importantly, they **must act as they are led by the Holy Spirit of God** in the matter. To obey is better than sacrifice; and, <u>***if you need help – ask for help from appropriate sources***</u>.

7) The group (or, person or persons) that we are dealing with are **not really here to worship** (they only use that as a pretext [alleged reason, ploy, excuse]; they really have other plans). Remember, we are in a <u>Great Controversy</u>, and we wrestle not against flesh and blood, but against principalities and powers in high places; in other words we are in a war against satan and his demons and their representatives! This is high level warfare!

> **"Can any man pick up a deadly serpent and not expect to be bit by it?**
> **Can you put burning coals in your breast and not be burnt?"**
> *(See Proverbs 6:27, 2, et cetera).*

Other Statements you could use:

(a) If these persons are convinced that their way is the right way (as much as we are of ours!), they should go and set up their own church / their own family (as we have!); a place where they can meet and have worship and fellowship with others that share their beliefs and teachings (as we are doing here!). ***How can two walk together except they are agreed?*** (Amos 3:3)

(b) Comparing the church to the family and, realizing the family is under threat of being broken up by the attack of persons from outside, coming in, pretending to be friends and family, pretending to have everything in common with the family and pretending to have the good of the family at heart, while planning to steal away the children, **is wrong** and <u>**cannot be tolerated!**</u>

(c) A good father (or mother) in any family under similar circumstance would **physically remove the threat**! Why should it be any different in the Church? Why should it be any different in <u>God's Church</u>? Why should it be any different in **this** church?

Getting Them Out of the Church: A Surgical Prescription

(Having said some or all of the above)

The Little Armageddon

Compare the leaders in the church to good fathers in the home, then state:
In this matter, the leaders have no choice but to ***physically*** remove the threat at this time… Why? Because as long as the threat (danger, risk, hazard) is present *in* the home there is a possibility of harm and danger and pain happening to the children - and possibly, even their death.

> (i) Hence, it cannot be any different in the Church of God - enough is enough (There is a time for everything – see Ecclesiastes 3). Point out that a really good father would not only ***physically remove*** the threat but would take steps to ***ensure that the threat does not re-enter the home***.

> (ii) Finally: The Rods normally attend the regular worship services of the church. During the service (especially Divine Service) identify and ask the person or persons or group identified as Shepherd's Rods to leave the church; if they do not leave on that request or directive *they should be escorted* (accompanied, guided, lead, ushered) out of the church building and ***off the church compound*** (by Deacons, Ushers, Leaders, Members).

Note Well:
Point out that they need to leave so that the service / worship can continue and that the service will not be resumed until they have either left or are escorted out.

Dear Leader in Zion: You might have the happy experience of them leaving even *before* you are through addressing the Church!

After they have left (or have been ushered out):

(iii) The deacons, ushers, leaders and membership at large should then be instructed ***not to allow them (the Rods) or any such like minded persons to come into the church in the future*** - because they are a part of a dangerous, divisive group that cannot be trusted and therefore should not be welcomed!

This strategy should ensure both the removal of the threat and, prevent it from re-entering the church family. Caution: In terms of preventing future incursions of the same Rods, the strategy will work *only if* the membership at large and the leaders of the church in particular, remain vigilant and take the appropriate action if / when they revisit the church, i.e.:

Repeat numbers (ii) and (iii) of the prescription - if necessary!

Be Vigilant my Brothers and Sisters! May the Lord judge between them and us.

A Template or Sample Letter

You were told earlier that notice should be given in writing. Here is a sample of how you could word your letter. Use the Church's Official Letterhead if you have one:

*A Sample Letter: *

Dear _____ (specific name or names or name of a family or person(s) involved or name of the offshoot group)

We have noticed that you (OR your family, etc.) have been visiting our church. It has been brought to the attention of the Church Board and the members of the church that you belong to one of the Shepherd's Rod groups. As such, your beliefs and teachings are contrary to what we, as Seventh-day Adventists believe. Furthermore, we are aware that the activities pursued by your group will cause disunity, apostasy and other problems in our church.

We are therefore requesting that you (OR "your family", etc.) do not visit this church (OR: write the name of the Church) in the future. At no time should you (OR your family, etc.) be seen on the church premises.

We hope you will give due consideration to our request and act accordingly, as failure to do so will result in action being taken to remove you from the Church premises.

Sincerely,

_____

(Preferably signed by one or more of the following: Church Clerk, Chairman of the Church Board, Elder(s), Head Deacon or other[s])

God be with you!

Can any reader need or want anything more? Well, if you do, it won't hurt to *keep reading*! We do have more! Please check out chapter eight!

Chapter Eight

Be Armed to the Teeth

For Good Measure: We Recommend that you be "Armed to the Teeth"!

Dear Reader, if you read the foregoing pages carefully and prayerfully you should have gotten the message, which is the intent of this manual: to show that Shepherd's Rods are dangerous and mean you and the church of which you are a part no good and that they are false teachers coming to really wreck your local church[21].

However, if you still need just a little more information and a little more clarity and a little more motivation here is:

A Layman's Commonsense Response to the Shepherd's Rod Problem and the Advice he Gave to the Members of His Local Church:

Identify Them!

The first thing you must realize is that there might be those in the church who just ***do not know*** the danger of

---

[21] No powers on earth can wreck "The Church of God" – but if you are not careful, your little (or big for that matter!) local congregation might be broken up if you do not act decisively. Can you take that risk?

The Little Armageddon

tolerating the Rods. So, be aware that opposition towards your seeking to prevent them from coming to your church is quite possible. Moreover, there is a possibility that someone in your church knows the individual(s) but is unaware that he / she is a member of the Shepherd's Rod group.

If you suspect someone to be a Shepherd's Rod one of the best ways to find out is to just use the ***direct approach***. Walk right up to him or her or them and just ask: "Are you (a) Shepherd's Rod(s)?" OR if you don't want to be that direct you could ask: "Where are you from?"; "What is your mission here?" Their answers to these questions – including non-verbal cues – should help you to make a determination as to whether or not they are *genuine* Seventh-day Adventists.

Also, bear in mind, if you are a Leader in the church: Shepherd's Rods usually hate or dislike Church Leaders (which suggests that the Rods have some *fear* of them) and, somewhere along the line this will come out, as they will try to turn the minds of members against the Leaders if they are allowed to stay in your church (leadership includes Pastors, Elders, The Conference, et cetera).

Be aware that they are most usually from "another church" (i.e. not a member of your local congregation) and they usually travel together (in pairs, fours or more!).

However, they will sit together or scatter as they see fit when they arrive at the church (they have learnt over the years to be as discreet as possible, especially if they suspect that they are expected at your church; in other words, over the years some of them have morphed – according to the past experiences they have had).

Rest assured dear reader that Shepherd's Rod ***do not*** work to win *new members* to the Church as Jesus commissioned us to do (See Matthew 28:18-20); they only work to corrupt the minds of *those already brought into the church by the efforts of others* who followed the great commission of Jesus Christ. In other words, they wouldn't be going out with you to do the regular evangelistic work of the church to lead the non-believer to Jesus (Sorry! No help from them to distribute handbills for an evangelistic meeting, no giving of Bible studies to prospective converts, et cetera). So, if there is a stranger or visitor at your church that claims to be a Seventh-day Adventist and do not take part in such activities…start asking questions or, at least start to take notice of what activities the individual do take part in and who they associate with; it's always better to be safe than sorry.

Remember (or be aware) also, if a Shepherd's Rod is standing and someone leading out asks that prayer be offered while everyone is standing they will (most likely) swiftly, and as discreetly as possible, fall to their knees while the prayer is going on (I say "most likely", because some of them are changing strategy or getting wise to this behaviour as an identifying mark and might resist kneeling at all times; in this they compromise on something that they firmly believe and when standing they would therefore feel they are being disobedient to their belief or, that they are less than perfect)

It bears repeating here that Shepherd's Rods are usually ***very stubborn*** and they are also ***very diligent*** in their subversive (mutinous, unruly, disobedient, insubordinate) work and will do whatever they can, whenever they can to advance their cause.

They also tend to be very arrogant (remember, they think they have "better light", "new light" or "higher light"; they believe that they are right – you are the one that is wrong!) and some even get downright rude (especially when they get frustrated by questions coming from a diligent, well informed, spiritual Church Leader!). You should expect them to speak down to you; you should expect them to speak to you with contempt. Be prepared to bear it by the grace of God!

More on where they are usually from: You will find that these persons are usually "former members" of some other local church than your own. In other words, they are usually persons that have been dis-fellowshipped from their home (or former) church usually because they have continued or persisted in their falsehood or false doctrines and were deemed to have apostatized.

Some might still be asking: But, how could they have been dis-fellowshipped or "read out" of their Church? What did they actually do to deserve that? As you will see below they can be dis-fellowshipped on the basis that they have abandoned their baptismal vows and / or have committed apostasy (fallen away from God's truth or, denounced the beliefs they once held).

It is extremely necessary and important that these questions be addressed because the Shepherd's Rods are usually adamant that they are (still) Seventh-day Adventists because they have (or had) done nothing wrong to be put out of their former Church! By this they imply that they should not be put out of this (present) church (that is, the church they are now "visiting"); they argue that the Leaders of their former church were just unfair to them and, were just very intolerant of different views.

The further implication is that the leaders at this church (your Local Church) should be more tolerant, fair-minded (or just) towards them than were the leaders in their former church.

The bottom-line for them is to achieve their objective of gaining sympathy and being allowed to <u>stay</u>; when this is achieved, they can continue their divisive activities without hindrance!

As stated earlier, Shepherd's Rods often claim that they were mistreated, misrepresented or otherwise unfairly treated when they were put out of their former church.

The question is:

Can their claim that they are Seventh-day Adventists be justified?

Was their former church wrong to throw them out? Should they really have been thrown out of the church (or disfellowshipped)? If yes, on what grounds?

We will answer these questions by doing a quick review of the Baptismal Vows that every person agrees to before being voted in as a member of the Seventh-day Adventist Church, subject to their baptism[22]. We will examine some of the vows carefully and compare them to some of the things the Shepherd's Rods believe, teach and practice[23] as a means of providing what I believe is incontrovertible justification for their excommunication from the church.

However, before we do that review, let's look at some of what the Church Manual says on the issues of disfellowshipping, <u>church membership</u>, baptismal covenant, et cetera:

22 A copy of the Baptismal Vows can easily be obtained – from the church manual, at the back of (some) baptismal certificates, et cetera.
23 In this section all emphases are mine.

From the Church Manual[24] under Church Membership, we read the following:

Membership on a Spiritual Basis

The serious, solemn obligations of church membership should be impressed on everyone who applies for admittance to the church. All should be faithfully taught what it means to become a member of the body of Christ. Only those giving evidence of having experienced the new birth, and who are enjoying a spiritual experience in the Lord Jesus, are prepared for acceptance into church membership. Thorough instruction in the fundamental teachings and related practices of the church should be given to every candidate for church membership before being baptized and received into church fellowship. Each person seeking admittance to the church should be informed of the principles for which the church stands.

"The members of the church, those whom He has called out of darkness into His marvelous light, are to show forth His glory. The church is the repository of the riches of the grace of Christ; and through the church will eventually be made manifest, even to 'the principalities and powers in heavenly places,' the final and full display of the love of God."—*The Acts of the Apostles*, p. 9.

Under *"Baptismal Covenant*[25]*"* we read the following:
A summary of doctrinal beliefs, prepared especially for the instruction of candidates for baptism, together with Baptismal Vow and Certificate of Baptism and Commitment, have been adopted by the denomination as a baptismal covenant. A printed copy of this covenant,

---
24 Seventh-day Adventist Church Manual, 17th Edition, Revised 2005, © 2005.
25 Ibidem p. 31

with the Certificate of Baptism and Commitment properly completed, should be furnished to all those who are accepted for church membership by baptism. In the case of those received on profession of faith, an appropriate certificate will also be given. This summary of doctrinal beliefs is especially prepared for the instruction of candidates for baptism. Each candidate should be thoroughly familiar with the teachings contained in this summary and with the duties enjoined upon believers and by practice demonstrate a willing acceptance of all the doctrines taught by Seventh-day Adventists and the principles of conduct which are the outward expression of these teachings, for it is "by their fruits ye shall know them." Prospective members of the Seventh-day Adventist Church, before baptism or acceptance on profession of faith, should be carefully instructed from the Scriptures in the fundamental beliefs of the church as presented in chapter 3 (see p. 9) of this *Church Manual*.

Under the heading "**Baptismal Vow and Baptism**[26]" we read: Candidates for baptism or those being received into fellowship by profession of faith shall affirm their acceptance of the doctrinal beliefs of the Seventh-day Adventist Church in the presence of the church or other properly appointed body. (See p. 31) The minister or elder should address the following questions to the candidate(s), whose reply may be by verbal assent or by raising the hand. *Vow*1. Do you believe…?" The vows are then listed.

So, dear reader, bear in mind throughout your reading of the rest of this chapter, that *the baptismal vows are based on what the Bible teaches* and what the Seventh-day Adventist Church believe, teach, practice and officially endorse as their *fundamental beliefs*. They are intended to be strictly held by the individual(s) who make the vows because the

---

26 Ibidem p. 32

renouncing of any *one* is tantamount to denial of the faith. Moreover, the renouncing of any *one* of these vows has very grave implications for *how a person will live his or her life* and also help to determine his or her attitude to the church. Finally, rejecting the vows will eventually determine his or her final destiny – whether it be eternal death or eternal life. So, dear friend, *this - is – **absolutely** - serious*.

Bear in mind also that in general a vow is a "**solemn pledge**: a promise to perform an act, carry out an activity, or behave in a given way"; specific to our context, it is a "**religious promise**: a solemn promise to join a religious order and live in accordance with its rules[27]."

So, vows are very important and one should endeavour to keep them. Persons who become Seventh-day Adventists are bound to their baptismal vows. The baptismal vows are vows made to the Lord and not to man. The fact that the vows are made by the individuals desiring membership in the church shows a commitment to start (or, having started) a ***relationship*** with the Lord. The Bible endorses the keeping of vows to the Lord. Numbers 30:2 says: "If a man vow a vow unto the LORD, or swear an oath to bind his soul with a bond; he shall not break his word, he shall do according to all that proceedeth out of his mouth."

With these in mind we will now do our comparison of the baptismal vows taken by an individual on entering into membership of the Seventh-day Adventist Church and the ideas, teachings and practices of the Shepherd's Rods.

---

[27] Microsoft® Encarta® 2007. © 1993-2006 Microsoft Corporation. All rights reserved.

Baptismal Vow # 5[28]:

"I believe that the Bible is **God's inspired Word**, and that it **constitutes the only rule of faith and practice** for the Christian."

This vow is based on the paramount fundamental belief from which all others flow and are grounded – *Fundamental belief number one:* **The Word of God:** "The Holy Scriptures, Old and New Testaments, are the written Word of God, given by divine inspiration through holy men of God who spoke and wrote as they were moved by the Holy Spirit"[29].

The Bible, God's Word, *is* truth (John 17:17) and Jesus is *the* truth (John 14:6). Only *truth* must be followed.

Dear Reader, please note:
The Shepherd's Rods will readily admit to you that the Bible is not their **only** rule of faith and practice. Why? Because they also believe, live by and teach the beliefs promulgated by Victor Tasho Houteff in his two-book volumes called "The Shepherd's Rod" and others of his writings!

This is because they believe that the writings of Victor Houteff are "God's inspired word". Hence, they virtually equate his teachings with scripture. In this little handbook you are now reading it has been *clearly established* that that claim *cannot be true*.

So, if Shepherd's Rods no longer subscribe to this vow… That's justification # 1 for dis-fellowshipping.

---

28 Ibidem p. 11.
29 *Seventh-day Adventists Believe, A Biblical Exposition of Fundamental Doctrines, p.9, Copyright 2005, Second Edition.*

Baptismal Vow # 7:

"I look forward to the soon coming of Jesus as the blessed hope in my heart, and I am determined to be ready to meet the Lord, and **to do all in my power to witness to His loving salvation**, and by life and word **to help others to be ready for His glorious appearing.**"

This vow is supported / based on at least three *fundamental beliefs*:

 # 11 Growing in Christ[30]: "No longer do we live in the darkness, fear of evil powers, ignorance, and meaninglessness of our former way of life. In this new freedom in Jesus, we are called to grow into the likeness of His character, communing with Him daily in prayer, feeding on His Word, meditating on it and on His providence, singing His praises, gathering together for worship, and **participating in the mission of the Church**.

 # 25 The Second Coming of Christ[31]: The second coming of Christ is the blessed hope of the church, the grand climax of **the gospel**.

 # 13 The Remnant and Its Mission[32]: The universal church is composed of all who truly believe in Christ, but in the last days, a time of widespread apostasy, a remnant has been called out to keep the commandments of God and the faith of Jesus. This remnant announces the arrival of the judgment hour, proclaims salvation through Christ, and heralds the approach of His second advent. This proclamation is symbolized by the three angels of Revelation 14; it coincides with the work of judgment in heaven and results in a work

---

30 Ibidem p. 149
31 Ibidem p. 371
32 Ibidem p.181

of repentance and reform on earth. **Every believer is called to have a personal part in this worldwide witness**.

Dear Reader, please note:
Part of growing in Christ is to participate in the mission of the church and the mission of the church is to take the gospel, the good news of salvation through Jesus Christ, to the world. The Seventh-day Adventist Church, being a peculiar movement, has a peculiar message to take to the world – and all who are so called must take part in the proclamation of the message.

As stated earlier, the Shepherd's Rod has abandoned this vow entirely and is only interested in getting persons that have already accepted the message of salvation and are preparing "for His glorious appearing" ***to come over to their side*** and to believe what they (the Shepherd's Rods) *now* believe, teach and practice. In other words, they are "*drawing away disciples unto themselves*" *rather than leading men to Jesus Christ and into the Church of God*, where they can "*be ready for His glorious appearing*". The Shepherd's Rods very clearly violate this vow!

Does the phrase "drawing away disciples unto themselves" sound familiar? That's because it is or, should be. You might have read it in Acts 20:28 – 30, a reference used earlier. ***Verse 30 says***: "Also of your own selves shall men arise, speaking perverse things, to draw away disciples after them." If we are to obey Jesus because we love Him (John 14:15) we must also take His commission in Matthew 28:19, 20 seriously and ***follow it***. We must share His burden for the salvation of souls; we must "go" as Jesus said – and tell everyone everywhere. Acts 1:8 says: "But ye shall receive power, after that the Holy Ghost is come upon you: and ye shall be witnesses unto me both in Jerusalem, and in all

The Little Armageddon

Judaea, and in Samaria, and unto the uttermost part of the earth." ***We must lead people to Jesus***. That, Dear Reader, is the essence of this Baptismal Vow; that is an ***imperative*** - and **the Shepherd's Rod unashamedly breaks this vow.**

That's justification # 2 for dis-fellowshipping.

Indeed, part of how we get ready for the blessed hope / second coming of Jesus is to be obedient / follow Jesus' footsteps and reflect His love that was manifested in His actions to save mankind. Jesus was a witness. We *must* be witnesses as well.

Baptismal Vow # 9:

"I believe in church organization, and it is my purpose to **support the church by my tithes and offerings**, and by **my personal effort and influence."**

This vow is supported or based on at least three *fundamental beliefs*, but principally belief # 21:

 # 12 The Church[33]: The church derives its authority from Christ, who is the incarnate Word, and from the Scriptures, which are the written Word. The church is God's family; adopted by Him as children, its members live on the basis of the new covenant. **The church is the body of Christ, a community of faith of which Christ Himself is the Head.**

 # 14 Unity in the Body of Christ[34]: **The church is one body with many members**, called from every nation, kindred, tongue, and people. Through the revelation of Jesus Christ in the Scriptures **we share the same faith and hope, and reach out in one witness to all.** This unity has

---
33 Ibidem p. 163.
34 Ibidem p. 201.

its source in the oneness of the triune God, who has adopted us as His children.

 # 21 Stewardship[35]: We are God's stewards, entrusted by Him with time and opportunities, abilities and possessions, and the blessings of the earth and its resources. We are responsible to Him for their proper use. **We acknowledge God's ownership by faithful service to Him and our fellow men, and by returning tithes and giving offerings for the proclamation of His gospel and the support and growth of His church.**

Dear Reader, please note:
As was pointed out earlier the lifework of the Shepherd's Rod is firmly hinged on divisiveness. They seek to tear down the church and build up themselves. Their work is a work of disunity and un-organization. They also do not usually return tithe and if / when they do its not to the Seventh-day Adventist Church but to their own organization – to strengthen and build it up to further proclaim their falsehoods.

Speak to Shepherd's Rods and it will come out very clearly that *they do not* "believe in church organization", i.e. **in the Seventh-day Adventist Church Organization (as implied in the vow)**; they do not like the church leadership and the church organization and **they do not return tithes and offerings to the Seventh-day Adventist Church!**[36] They also certainly **do not** (or, **no longer**) support the church **by their personal effort and influence**! Instead, they are, by their concerted and determined efforts, doing the very opposite! They are seeking to break down the church organization by their personal influence and

35 Ibidem p.301.
36 This was very clearly pointed out in Chapter Three in the article: "Who Are The Davidian Seventh-day Adventists?"

effort! They are actually seeking to (or, some would say has) create an organization (or church) within the church (or organization). By their efforts they are causing *disunity* in the body of Christ. In fact, if their efforts were allowed to go <u>unchecked</u> they would run amuck and *totally wreck the church / organization*! It would be **bedlam** indeed!!

Let's go to the *Church Manual*:

Self-appointed Organizations—The church in its organized capacity is God's instrumentality for preserving order and discipline among His people. Its God-given message is borne to the world not only by the personal testimony of the individual member but in the corporate witness of the church as the body of Christ. Such corporate witness requires the recognized administrative structure that has been established with all duly elected officers and all properly organized channels of work such as the Sabbath School, Personal Ministries, Youth organizations, et cetera. It also acknowledges such self-supporting institutions whose activities contribute to the attainment of the church's objectives. Therefore, although all members have equal rights within the church, no individual member or group of members should start a movement or form an organization or seek to encourage a following for the attainment of any objective or for the teaching of any doctrine or message not in harmony with the fundamental religious objectives and teachings of the Seventh-day Adventist Church. Such a course would result in the fostering of a factional and divisive spirit, in the fragmenting of the effort and witness of the church, and thus in hindering it in the discharge of its obligations to its Head and to the world. ***Seventh-day Adventist Church Manual, Revised 2005, 17th Edition, p. 190.***

Under **Reasons for Which Members Shall Be Disciplined** in the Church Manual, the ninth one listed states:

"Persistent <u>refusal</u> to recognize properly constituted church authority or to submit to the order and discipline of the church." p. 195.

Also, the eighth on the list states:

"Adhering to or taking part in a divisive or disloyal movement or organization."

So, dear friend, the Shepherd's Rods cannot be allowed to continue their divisive activities in the Church…not in *your* church!

If the violation of this vow and its implications is not clear…I – don't – know – what – is!

That's justification # 3 for dis-fellowshipping.

Dear Reader, are you still wondering? Is there or, are there ground(s) to dis-fellowship the Church member that has decided to embrace the teachings of the Shepherd's Rod group?

Well, whether or not you do, please keep reading:

Baptismal Vow # 11:

"I know and understand the **fundamental Bible principles as taught by the Seventh-day Adventist Church**. It is my purpose, by the grace of God, to **order my life in harmony with these principles**."

Since the fundamental beliefs of the Seventh-day Adventist Church are all based on the Word of God, clearly, this vow is based on / refers to all the fundamental beliefs and asks

The Little Armageddon

the convert / member to live in harmony with the principles contained in those beliefs.

Dear reader, please note:
The truth is that **the Shepherd's Rod orders his or her life according to principles taught by Victor Houteff** and not (only) those taught by the Seventh-day Adventist Church; they demonstrate this very well *by teaching from Houteff's writings and trying to persuade others to follow them*. While they (still) hold some of the beliefs of the Seventh-day Adventist Church, the typical Shepherd's Rod is proud of his or her knowledge of the teachings of Victor Houteff and, believes and follows them. Moreover, by following Houteff's teachings they are certainly **not** sticking to *the "fundamental Bible principles* as taught by the Seventh-day Adventist Church." Why? Because some of Houteff's teachings (as shown above) are *totally contrary* to what Seventh-day Adventists believe and teach. The truth is, some of what Houteff wrote seems to be nothing but figments.

Under **Reasons for Which Members Shall Be Disciplined** in the Church Manual, the first one on the list states:

"Denial of faith in the fundamentals of the gospel and in the cardinal doctrines of the church or teaching doctrines contrary to the same. " p. 195.

The fact is that many Shepherd's Rods will tell you that **they endorse (and teach) several other, so called, "fundamental Bible principles"** that the Seventh-day Adventist Church does not endorse or teach (Of course, these are a part of *their* **false teachings,** as clearly shown earlier, that originated with Victor Tasho Houteff – but, primarily, I believe, - *in the mind of Satan himself*!).

Under **Reasons for Which Members Shall Be Disciplined** in the Church Manual, the second one listed states:

"Violation of the law of God, such as worship of idols, murder, stealing, profanity, gambling, Sabbathbreaking, and *willful and habitual falsehood*. " Now, that's really, really clear!

That's justification # 4 for dis-fellowshipping.

If that is still not enough, please check out the following:

Baptismal Vow # 13:

"**I accept that the Seventh-day Adventist Church is *the remnant church* of Bible prophecy**, and that people of every nation, race, and language are invited and accepted into its **fellowship**. I desire to be a member in this local congregation of the world church."

This is clearly based on fundamental belief # 13 (see above under Baptismal Vow # 7).

Dear reader, please note:
God has *one true remnant church* that keeps the commandments of God and has the testimony of Jesus Christ (Rev. 12:17). There is only *one* church. There is absolutely no "church within the church". The church is one united entity not a fragmented and disunited body.

The Shepherd's Rods have *outrightly rejected* this vow. They do not (any longer) accept that the Seventh-day Adventist Church is **the** Remnant Church; if they did they would not be in violation of the baptismal vows listed here! And, they most certainly have been in violation! Also, they would not be seeking to make *"a remnant of the remnant"* OR *"a remnant within the remnant"*. This demonstrates that they want to remake the Remnant Church to fit into their view of what the Remnant Church should be and do (or teach) OR to convert all the church to their side. By doing that they certainly demonstrate that they do not desire any "*fellowship*" (companionship, association, friendship) with the true Remnant Church of God! They confirm this by actively recruiting members of the church to join <u>them</u>. Why do they do that? Because they believe and teach that <u>they</u> are the *true remnant* with the true, higher, better light. Consequently, they are very arrogant. In essence then (in reality), by their own attitude and actions, ***they dis-fellowship themselves***! So, they are really **lying** when they claim to be Seventh-day Adventists because, since they have renounced these vows – they most certainly are **not** Seventh-day Adventists!

For this one there is absolutely no question – given their stance on this one, they embrace being "thrown out" of the church (being disfellowshipped); for them, it's like getting a badge of honour.

That's justification # 5 for dis-fellowshipping.

With so much talk about disfellowshipping so far, let us look at what the Church Manual says about the matter. This will serve to bolster and expound some of what has been said.

Under *Church Discipline, page 187*[37] we read:

"As those thus united in Christian fellowship offer prayer to God and pledge themselves to deal justly, to love mercy, and to walk humbly with God, great blessing comes to them. If they have wronged others they continue the work of repentance, confession, and restitution, fully set to do good to one another. This is the fulfilling of the law of

---
37 *Ibidem* - Seventh-day Adventist Church Manual…

Christ. " 'But if he will not hear thee, then take with thee one or two more, that in the mouth of two or three witnesses every word may be established.' Matthew 18:16. Take with you those who are spiritually minded, and talk with the one in error in regard to the wrong. He may yield to the united appeals of his brethren. As he sees their agreement in the matter his mind may be enlightened. " 'And if he shall neglect to hear them,' what then shall be done? Shall a few persons in a board meeting take upon themselves the responsibility of disfellowshipping the erring one? 'If he shall neglect to hear them, tell it unto *the church.*' Verse 17. Let the church take action in regard to its members."—*Testimonies,* vol. 7, p. 262. " 'But if he neglect to hear the church, let him be unto thee as an heathen man and a publican.' Verse 17. If he will not heed the voice of the church, if he refuses all the efforts made to reclaim him, upon the church rests the responsibility of separating him from fellowship. His name should then be stricken from the books.

"No church officer should advise, no committee should recommend, nor should any church vote, that the name of a wrong doer shall be removed from the church books, until the instruction given by Christ has been faithfully followed. When this instruction has been followed, the church has cleared herself before God. The evil must then be made to appear as it is, and must be removed, that it may not become more and more widespread. The health and purity of the church must be preserved, that she may stand before God unsullied, clad in the robes of Christ's righteousness. . . ." 'Verily I say unto you,' Christ continued, 'whatsoever ye shall bind on earth shall be bound in heaven: and whatsoever ye shall loose on earth shall be loosed in heaven.' Verse 18. "This statement holds its force in all ages. On the church has been conferred the power to act in Christ's stead. It is God's instrumentality

for the preservation of order and discipline among His people. To it the Lord has delegated the power to settle all questions respecting its prosperity, purity, and order. Upon it rests the responsibility of excluding from its fellowship those who are unworthy, who by their un-Christlike conduct would bring dishonor on the truth. Whatever the church does that is in accordance with the directions given in God's word will be ratified in heaven."—*Testimonies*, vol. 7, pp. 262, 263. (Italics supplied.)

"The Lord desires His followers to exercise great care in dealing with one another. They are to lift up, to restore, to heal. But there is to be in the church no neglect of proper discipline. The members are to regard themselves as pupils in a school, learning how to form characters worthy of their high calling. In the church here below, God's children are to be prepared for the great reunion in the church above. Those who here live in harmony with Christ may look forward to an endless life in the family of the redeemed."—*Testimonies*, vol. 7, pp. 263, 264.

Under the topic: ***Church Responsible for Dealing With Sin*** we read: God holds His people, as a body, responsible for the sins existing in individuals among them. If the leaders of the church neglect to diligently search out the sins which bring the displeasure of God upon the body, they become responsible for these sins."—*Testimonies*, vol. 3, p. 269.

"He would teach His people that disobedience and sin are exceedingly offensive to Him, and are not to be lightly regarded. He shows us that when His people are found in sin they should at once take decided measures to put that sin from them that His frown may not rest upon them all. But if the sins of the people are passed over by those in responsible positions, His frown will be upon them, and the people of God, as a body, will be held responsible for those sins. *Testimonies*, vol. 3, pp. 265.

Unconsecrated Resist Church Discipline—"There are many who do not have the discretion of Joshua and who have no special duty to search out wrongs and to deal promptly with the sins existing among them. Let not such hinder those who have the burden of this work upon them; let them not stand in the way of those who have this duty to do. Some make it a point to question and doubt and find fault because others do the work that God has not laid upon them. These stand directly in the way to hinder those upon whom God has laid the burden of reproving and correcting prevailing sins in order that His frown may be turned away from His people. Should a case like Achan's be among us, there are many who would accuse those who might act the part of Joshua in searching out the wrong, of having a wicked, faultfinding spirit. God is not to be trifled with and His warnings disregarded with impunity by a perverse people. "I was shown that the manner of Achan's confession was similar to the confessions that some among us have made and will make. They hide their wrongs and refuse to make a voluntary confession until God searches them out, and then they acknowledge their sins. A few persons pass on in a course of wrong until they become hardened. They may even know that the church is burdened, as Achan knew that Israel were made weak before their enemies because of his guilt. Yet their consciences do not condemn them. They will not relieve the church by humbling their proud, rebellious hearts before God and putting away their wrongs. God's displeasure is upon His people, and He will not manifest His power in the midst of them while sins exist among them and are fostered

The Little Armageddon

by those in responsible positions. "Those who work in the fear of God to rid the church of hindrances and to correct grievous wrongs, that the people of God may see the necessity of abhorring sin and may prosper in purity, and that the name of God may be glorified, will ever meet with resisting influences from the unconsecrated."—*Testimonies*, vol. 3, pp. 270, 271.

So, expect opposition.

I hope I have given a clear enough exposition of this matter. I hope you now see more clearly why the Shepherd's Rods have been *dis-fellowshipped* (i.e. put out of fellowship) from the church. If they are no longer of the same persuasion as us there is no point in having them continuing with us; there is really no fellowship as the relationship changes once certain beliefs are rejected. In essence, once truth is rejected and falsehood is embraced one is really living in disobedience or practicing iniquity (which is lawlessness).

Of course, the normal process of dis-fellowshipping a believer is usually followed - as they would or should be for any other reason for dis-fellowshipping. Especially in these cases persons are usually counseled or advised; studies are usually done with them and generally, efforts are made towards reconciliation. Disfellowshipping is never something that the church hurriedly embraces.

Hence, the leaders in the churches have <u>every right</u> to put them out of the church as soon as they have been identified!

Dear reader, God's church is **one body**. He is the head (Ephesians 4:4 - 6). It is quite possible for someone to claim to be a Seventh-day Adventist and claim to have "higher light" and a "better understanding" of God's words **and be**

lost! So, what we are examining is a tremendously serious issue! Surely, Matthew 7:21 - 23 could also apply to the members of this group as long as **they do not change and return to the fold of God's True Remnant Church**. It could likewise apply to any one else (any of us) that has even one sin that is cherished and / or un-confessed! So, don't feel too self-righteous and start suffering from the "I am better than they are" syndrome! I beg you to keep looking to Jesus! I will be following my own advice.

Note:

The exposition on the fundamental beliefs shows clearly that the Rods have "*given up the faith*" or apostatized with respect to a number of those beliefs. That is sure grounds for excommunication from church membership or fellowship. Shepherd's Rods set themselves up as the reformers and purifiers of the Seventh-day Adventist Church. They think *themselves* to be more good and righteous and pure than everyone else in the church (That reminds me of the Pharisees of Jesus' day). They feel that the leaders of the church are corrupt and that the Conference is not using God's money (the tithe) properly (hence, they do not return tithe to the church but to their own group – to finance their activities, and so on). They also believe that there are many other "fundamental beliefs" that the Seventh-day Adventist Church should be teaching and that these are an expression of what constitutes "higher light" (Which are really the teachings of Victor Houteff – the false prophet! When I really think of it, knowing that those teachings are spurious, I believe they are rather obnoxious in stating or believing such). They believe that they have this "higher light" and are prepared to teach it. As far as they are concerned they just need to be given a chance to do so freely – in any Seventh-day Adventist Church they choose to. **God forbid!!!** The

The Little Armageddon

founder of the group was excommunicated for persistently teaching the said falsehoods. It will be the same for those who persistently teach and follow the same falsehoods today. On the basis of what was presented above, **<u>I absolutely agree</u>**.

Brothers and sisters, when Jesus was sending out His disciples He cautioned them: "Behold, I send you forth as sheep in the midst of wolves: be ye therefore wise as serpents, and harmless as doves". If we find ourselves in the midst of wolves (Matthew 7:15) - even within the church - may we be found to be wise! (Proverbs 9:10, James 1:5).

Rejecting the vows and the underlying fundamental beliefs contained in them speaks to a loss of or deterioration of the relationship with Jesus Christ as Saviour and Lord. ***That is the crux of the matter.***

You may also do well to consider the following quote as an extra piece in your armour:

"Those who are inclined to regard their individual judgment as supreme are in grave peril. It is Satan's studied effort to separate such ones from those who are channels of light, through whom God has wrought to build up and extend His work in the earth. To neglect or despise those whom God has appointed to bear the responsibilities of leadership in connection with the advancement of the truth, is to reject the means that He has ordained for the help, encouragement, and strength of His people. For any worker in the Lord's cause to pass these by, and **to think that his light must come through no other channel than directly from God, is to place himself in a position where he is liable to be deceived by the enemy and overthrown**. The Lord in His wisdom has arranged that by means of the close relationship that should be maintained by all believers, Christian shall be united to Christian and church to church. Thus the human instrumentality will be enabled to co-operate with the divine. **Every agency will be subordinate to the Holy Spirit, and all the believers will be united in an organized and well-directed effort to give to the world the glad tidings of the grace of God.** {AA 164.1}

While the Shepherd's Rods pride themselves in knowing the Spirit of Prophecy writings they have in thought, word and action rejected counsel like this. Hence, they are totally deceived by Satan and believe and practice lies.

God has the remedy for all our problems. He has the remedy for our *sin* problem – because "the blood of Jesus Christ his Son cleanseth us from all sin." (1 John1:7). God keeps us as "the apple of His eye" (Deuteronomy 32:10, Zechariah 2:8). **His church will triumph!** Let's stand with the Lord in this battle.

Time to take some well needed rest in Jesus.

Praise the Lord!

The Little Armageddon

Unless you have unction; unless you really know God; unless you are controlled by the Holy Spirit you will not have the discernment, you will not have the ability to truly see; you will be unable to identify the enemy.

How absolutely pivotal it is for us to identify the enemy in our battles. If we cannot identify the enemy how will we be able to fight? If we do not recognize the enemy, the enemy could be right among us and we do not know. That could be a fatal error. If we are unable to see the enemy for what he is we will be destroyed; totally *consumed* by the enemy! Sobriety and vigilance is very necessary.

1 John 2:17 – 20 / 1 Peter 5:8

Chapter Nine

Experience Teaches Wisdom! Personal Experiences From A Veteran Warrior in the Battle of the Little Armageddon

I have the privilege to know a very battle-ready soldier in God's army who gave me a very strong foundation in God's words through his constant teaching and guidance as he nurtured me as a baby Christian. He has been a very positive influence and a real mentor to me. Even today I am still positively influenced and inspired by his dedication and zeal for the work of God – even after over thirty years of being an active member of the Seventh-day Adventist Movement. He was interviewed in order to get additional insight into the strategies of the Shepherd's Rod offshoots and how to deal with them.

Interview[38]:

---

38 This represents excerpts from a taped interview with Elder David Swaby done on Tuesday January 4, 2005. After I thought I had finished writing the book I was encouraged by the Holy Spirit to go and have this interview done. I had the distinct impression that it would help to strengthen the case for those who are on the Lord's side and, help dispel some doubts from the hearts of the yet undecided in the battle. of the *Little Armageddon*. Included here by his kind and enthusiastic permission.

The Little Armageddon

First Experience:

JC: What are your first experiences with Shepherd's Rods (SR)?

DS: Some were at the North Street Church. **They would have meetings and go around and invite people to the meetings**. They pretended they were just doing lesson studies … but they were SR. While they were conducting their meetings **they would visit the church and distribute their tracts to the members** when church is dismissed. I was a young man in the church but at the time I happened to be one of those who would go around and discourage the members from taking the tracts, realizing that they were very dangerous. They continued their work and their group grew and grew. **Many men who I went in the church and saw became SR**.

Exodus From The Church and Impact of the SR on a Young Church

JC: So, many of them left the church?

DS: Yes. I left from that church and started attending my present church when it was just a little Company… in a little bamboo shed. There were not many SR at that time. One or two would come in but they weren't so much of a problem. As soon as the church was properly built and established they started to attend and **members from the church started to "take side" with them**. This continued for a while, until **when we were having crusades the SR would come in and work with some of the <u>new converts</u> and encourage them to go with them to their meetings** so they can "teach them to be better Christians".

John Churchill

The Elder's Response and A Massive SR Invasion

JC: What was your response to this situation?
DS: At that time I was very much *"on the ball"* and, with other members of the church, we worked strong to keep the members from being led astray. It so happened that on one occasion; this was the biggest attack; there was a large vacant lot a short distance up the road from the church; a group of the SR came to the church …we didn't know there were so many until later; a large group of them came to the church!

JC: Like … how many of them?
DS: Plenty!

JC: You mean like a bus-load?
DS: Busloads and carloads of them! And it was so shocking to the people next door to the church…because they wanted to know what was happening…because normally, when we were going to have big meetings…they would know from the Friday night so they would come and fix up the place (i.e. the church). It so happened that they (the SR) wanted to come into the church and the deacons took control and didn't allow them in; but, at that time, members of the church were members of the SR group so, they wanted them to come in. So, one of our deacons went to the police station and let the police know we were having a problem at the church…and the Sergeant came up to the church. He asked them what they were doing there … so, they said they were Seventh-day Adventists and we were not allowing them into the church; the police then told me what they said; so, the Sergeant told them that we (leaders and members) have the authority to decide who we want to come in or, not come in to the church and he cannot tell us to let them in; he said we could even stop him (the police)…except if there is any

offence committed, he could come in…by force if necessary. So, they (the SR) went away.

JC: Before the police came, did they try to put up any *physical* resistance? OR, push their way into the church?
DS: When you say physical (pause). Technically, they wanted to use force; they wanted to push their way to come … that's why the deacons took control of the gate … until the police came.

JC: Where was the Pastor at the time? Were you alone?
DS: At that time, the Pastor wasn't there.

JC: Who was the Pastor?
DS: Pastor __ __ Brown.

JC: He was the one who baptized me, you know.
DS: Yes; good; but he was out of the area at the time.
JC: Okay.
DS: And, people were saying: The Pastor gone away and leave the Elder (D.S. - laughing) alone to manage, but the Elder manage! (D.S. - more laughing). He (the Pastor) was surprised, you know; because when the Pastor came he heard what had happened.
DS: And so, they were out.
DS: Well, we had one or two of them that used to attend the church; we never stopped those from attending.

Sabbath School Time

JC: Okay.
DS: But, we always had lesson review at Sabbath School; and so, there were two of them that were there that I knew personally, from another church. But during the lesson review when they put their hand up to ask questions I didn't allow them to do so at that time.

JC: Why not? If you allowed them to talk, what would they do?
DS: Depending on the lesson, they would try to swing it away from our doctrine to suit their doctrine…and so, I didn't allow them to talk.

JC: If you allowed them to talk, would they try to take over the Sabbath School?
DS: Yes; if you allow them; because **they would try to talk for a long time, to push their side**; and so, they found out that they could not get through. One of them approached me one day and said: You know me from so long ago when we used to be at our other church, and you wouldn't even allow me to ask a question.

JC: What did you say to him?
DS: I knew you when you were a "good-good" Seventh-day Adventist…but now you are a Shepherd's Rod (D.S. - laughingly) and I can't let you speak (laughingly); I just can't allow you to talk (D.S. - healthy laughter).

What was special about the SR? / Twisting Ellen White's writing

JC: What is special about the SR? What is it that makes them want to come and push their brand of teaching on the church?
DS: They have some kind of doctrines…I can't even remember them because I never really tried to digest them… but, what they do mostly is to **quote a lot from Ellen G. White's writings.**

JC: Yes?
DS: And, of course, **many of the members never knew anything about Ellen White.**

JC: Okay.
DS: And so, **they would twist (*the quotes*) their way.**

A Very Wicked Strategy of the SR

JC: Alright.
DS: They did that to attract the people, and that's the reason why, **when we have crusades and they see the people baptized, they work along with them to pull them away.**

JC: So, they actually observe those that are attending the baptismal classes and then target them after baptism?
DS: Yes. We had a big crusade and many persons were baptized and, fortunately, **I was very watchful** and, when I missed some members one Sabbath, I went and found them the same Saturday night; I went to all of them and asked them where they were. They said that some brethren from another church came and took them in vehicles (the SR had told them to meet at a certain place); they picked up a van-load (*of Church members*) and took them somewhere off Waltham Park Road, where they had projector, screens, and so on, set up to attract the people, gave them nice lunch, et cetera. However, **I worked with those brethren and they stopped attending the meetings**; so, they never got them again (laughingly); so, they never got anybody from my church!

JC: So, they did not ever get anyone from your church?
DS: No. I know of two or three persons that were at the church; I do not know what strategy the SR used to win them, but they became SR (before coming to this church) and, they were usually at the church but I was not vexed with them. I was very friendly with them; some church members used to say how it is I am so friendly with them.

They (the SR) might be able to put in a lie or two – but not everything they say will be a lie.

Strategies of the SR Identified by the Elder

JC: Over the years, what have you found out that they do to "win" people?
DS: (1) They would quote the **Spirit of Prophecy** their way (to suit themselves), (2) Take people to their places and have **film shows** that sound like truth; but on further investigation one can establish that they are not true, (3) They would **talk about health**.

JC: Health? O-kay.
DS: They would talk about what we are eating and what we shouldn't be eating, et cetera, and, by that means get the people. They were very influential with that.

SR Who Came Back to the Fold?

JC: Do you know any SR's that were very active, recruiting people, et cetera, that have come back into the Seventh-day Adventist Church?
DS: Do you mean drop out of the SR and come back to the fold?

JC: Yes, do you know of any?
DS: Yes, I have heard of about three of them – but not in Jamaica.

JC: Not in Jamaica? So, you don't personally or directly know of any?
DS: No. But I know of some who were very active but they now "keep cool" or, are not active anymore.

JC: They "toned down"?

The Little Armageddon

DS: They were very active and hot but they suddenly just "cool down"[39].

Could You Know the Shepherd's Rods?

JC: How widely known was the group? Would the general membership know that they are around?
DS: Well, according to their appearance you could know them.

JC: How could you know them?
DS: Apart from those of us who would know them from long ago…sometimes they meet people when the church service is over and try to take them away from the crowd and tell them about Ellen G. White and the things she said or tell them they would give them studies or, plan with them to go to their homes and give them studies.

SR Literature Distribution Strategy

JC: Do they usually have literature?
DS: Yes; they would have literature and other things with them. I used to have some of their materials. A group of the SR used to write to me.

JC: Write to you?
DS: Yes, and send a lot of materials to me…and they found out that (D.S. - laughing) they could not convince me.

JC: How would they distribute the literature that they have with them when they come to church?
DS: If ten of them came they would have a certain amount of literature (each of them)…as you exit the church they would give you one.

---

39 Author's note: These were the same persons referred to earlier as ones with whom he was friendly. It was his actions that actually caused them to "cool down".

JC: Do you know of any of them leaving the literature on the seats?

DS: Yes, some would leave it around, because they know that members will take them up…because they tried to be as disguised as possible so you wont identify them as going the wrong way; they leave it on the seat, so a member might take it up thinking it's literature from the church and read it…but some just gave it to you personally. When I was at another Church they would go out on the road when church is over and as the members are coming out of the church service they would just give them the literature.

Do the SR Approach Non-SDA's?

JC: Do they approach people who are not Seventh-day Adventist?

DS: No. No, no. **Their work is just to pull people out of the Adventist Church**. They say a few will be saved, and although the church is Seventh-day Adventist Church but, many inside the church will be lost…most of them…because they are not doing what God says.

JC: So, in other words (have you heard the phrase)…they are saying that "a remnant out of a remnant" will be saved?

DS: Yes, that's what they use…I heard about some of our brothers and sisters that went over to them (some I came in the church and saw).

Have Any Church Leaders Become Shepherd's Rods?

JC: Like what level members? You mean just ordinary members? Do you know of leaders that have gone over to them?

DS: Yes, I know of Elders that have gone over to them.

JC: Elders!?

DS: Yes Elders!

JC: Do you know of any Pastors?
DS: I have heard it ... but I can't prove it.

JC: You have just heard it?
DS: Yes, I've just heard so too.

SR Offering to Help Members

JC: I have heard of them offering to help members with jobs, schooling, etc. ... have you ever heard of any such thing?
DS: Yes, yes .. they do. They do everything possible to attract people. I know one brother (a SR) that *was living* at Papine. I came and found them here at this church. He was doing a lot of things to help people.

Insisting on Kneeling to Pray

JC: Is dropping to their knees to pray or, not standing when praying or when prayer is being offered a telltale sign for SR?
DS: When I just came in the church, attending a church in Kingston some SR came to me and said, young man!, when they say pray, you <u>must</u> kneel ... and they followed me with that; but it so happened that I went to the Lay Preachers' Institute and, when I returned, the Sabbath, after service (Divine Hour) dismissed (the person leading out had said let us stand for prayer – so I stood) ... a group of them came to me and said young man!, what are you doing? You <u>must</u> kneel ... you <u>must</u> kneel, the Bible says kneel. I said to them (I was glad I was in the army) ... I said to them ... okay. (That was before I had gone to Lay Preachers' Institute). So, I started to kneel with them too. However, they have a rule in the army which says you must comply with orders and

then complain later. So, I said, I have been complying and not complaining. So, I went and complained to the Pastor.

JC: Yes (!?).
DS: And the Pastor told me … for the benediction, you can stand … and he explained that even sometimes at Divine Hour, if the place is not convenient, etc. you can stand. He explained everything to me … and then I said, I complied and complained and now I have the information, so I won't be kneeling again. Then, the SR said: But young man – you must obey orders! I said, yes, I must obey what *thus saith the Lord*! And I started to show them how I went to the leader of the church … who are like the officers in the army – they are in charge … and they give command and we must comply … and complain after. (JC: Was very amused with the account)

The greatest defense against the SR?

JC: What would you say is the greatest defense against the SR?
DS: Firstly, remember that when they want to study with you, they want to do it *privately* … not publicly … and not at the church either. They have places where they want you to go … **DO NOT GO to any secret place with them** away from the church. There are officers in the church; when they called me to go and study with them I went to the officers of the church and told them who have invited me to study with them and asked what I should do. The leaders then advised me. That is why I never got trapped by them! The leaders explained to me … so, when they came to me (about always kneeling) and says you're disobedient … and that's what God said … I told them that's what THEY said, not God. (JC: Was very amused at this juncture)

The Little Armageddon

Should we Study Their Doctrines?

JC: Would you say that we should study their doctrines?
DS: Listen. As a true Seventh-day Adventist I don't have to study their doctrines.

JC: What should we do?
DS: We have the word of God for ourselves to study - to guide us.

JC: So, we should study the genuine doctrines?
DS: Sure. I don't need to go into any corner with them for them to study to give me any ideas.

Soldier, be alert! Heads up!

I want my readers to take very careful note of the following:

Mixing Truth and Error

DS: Mind you, I am not saying that everything they say is wrong ... because, if they said everything wrong they would not be succeeding ... but they tell you some things that are correct ... but...I don't want the wrong and good mixed together ... so, I keep out of their way. I rebel against them, and they don't have anything to tell me privately (anything they are going to tell me) I can study for myself. Also, we have leaders of the church – good, dedicated, sincere leaders I can go to for help and instruction.

What Has Kept Them Going?

JC: Why do you think this group has persisted over the years?
DS: Some of the things they teach, that's why they are still going on. For example, they say "many are called but few

are chosen" ... that's what some say ... and they (the Rods) are the few (DS: Chuckles); they are the chosen ones; that's what they say ... and because they say that people tend to believe; and some of them (those who believe them) after they get trapped into it and they find they were wrong they are ashamed to leave the group.

JC: Oh, so they end up staying?
DS: Yes, they just stay ... but they play the game ... they are no longer with them ... but they answer the calls with them[40].

Heads up again, soldier!

Advice to New Converts and Others[41]

JC: Is there any advice you would give to new converts and young Seventh-day Adventist Christians?
DS: Not only to young ones alone, but to every Seventh-day Adventist ... but especially the younger ones just coming in, not only by age, but if you're just coming in the fold; when you are invited by any individual or group to go and study with them ... since you are just coming in the church, go to the leaders of the church and ask them: brother so and so, or, sister so and so asked me to go to their house to study: should I go? And they will advise you.

Study the Word of God

JC: To guard against getting caught up in false teachings would you say that they (new Christians) need to really study the doctrines of the church?

---

40 Doesn't this sound like those that will receive the mark of the beast in their hand?
41 For this bit of advice to be good to follow it is absolutely imperative that the leadership of the Church be aware and knowledgeable of the SR and other offshoots.

The Little Armageddon

DS: Yes, we need to study. Study for yourselves; "study to show thyself approved"; study; mind you (be careful) you know, they might give you some materials to study that are correct right through ... but that is ... that is the bait! (DS: Chuckling and laughing!).

JC: O – kay!
DS: You see, that's the bait (DS: Chuckling again).

JC: So, they will give you something that has no fault in it?
DS: ... no fault in it...

JC: Maybe, then afterwards ...
DS: ... and, they gradually ... bring in their false teachings.

JC: But that can be rather dangerous!
DS: Yes, it's dangerous.

JC: Because, remember, with the serpent and Eve it was just one word ...
DS: Yes...

JC: ... it (the serpent) changed...
DS: So, they are very tactful with that. They'll tell you the truth ... they'll say, yes, that is truth, this is also truth ... but a little after, when you get into them, they pull you by giving you a touch here and a touch there, piece by piece (of their false doctrines) 'til they have you full! (JC: Couldn't stop the laugh from flowing out like water at this juncture!)

**The devil is Busy and, ready to Destroy –
But Time Will Soon be Up For him**

JC: Hmm, hmm!
JC: Is there anything else that you want to say?

DS: I would say right now, you know, we are in the last days and the devil is ***on his toes***. Its like when you are playing a football (soccer) match and the game is at one all (1 – 1) and there is ten minutes to go … you know the whistle can blow at any time … you are hot on the scene, you are doing everything possible to score that one other goal. The devil knows that we are in the very last … the last events now … ***he knows*** … and he knows that his time is coming to an end … and he agrees to himself that he alone is not going … he is going to carry down as much as possible with him. He has no more chance, and he is doing everything possible and, not because a person is a Pastor or an Elder, or an old time member of the church we should say "he's safe" … he (*satan*) is working on everybody!

JC: Everybody?

DS: Yes, everybody; and he knows that it is easier to blindfold those that are just coming in … but he is also working with the senior members of the church too. Don't be surprised that a Pastor or Elder gone on that side. Some might not go fully … but they are doing a little touch of it too. So, you have to look out for anything right now. I want us to realize that we are in ***the last days*** and the devil is doing everything possible … to catch us. He knows that many of us will not go outside and curse (bad words) and drink alcoholic beverages (rum, beer, et cetera) so, he says, okay; but, I am going to use this now … see the truth here; come this way.

This interview has certainly blessed and strengthened me. It contains very, very valuable counsel regarding the Shepherd's Rod group and how we should relate to them. We are truly in the **time of the end**. Soon, my friend, it will be **the end of time**. **Be ready!**

The Little Armageddon

Interview Postscript:

DS: I used to get plenty materials from some of them. They used to write to me and tell me things. Years ago, when I was the Lay Activities Leader, I used to write abroad and I would get a lot of tracts and magazines for the church through the post[42]. They were very smart; they used to send a lot of their tracts for me along with the other magazines and tracts. Sometimes two or three hundred magazines and tracts would come. I *wouldn't* just take them to the church but searched them … sometimes I would find some of their tracts inside of / between the other good tracts and magazines (chuckle). I would just take them out … and dump them. They would send Review and Herald, et cetera, but send their books in between. After a while I would have a whole heap to just burn. So, they are very tactful.

Interview conducted: Tuesday, January 4, 2005, 7:00 – 8:00 p.m.

In any warfare weaponry is crucial to victory or defeat. Superior weaponry introduced at the right time has turned the tides in many wars, some of which were of almost global proportions (The US's entrance into WWI and WWII comes readily to my mind).

Personally, I do not think the battle of the *Little Armageddon* – nor, for that matter, Armageddon (the climaxing conflict in the Great Controversy / the war between the forces of good and evil) - is a fair battle! It certainly is ***not fair*** – it is not fair for Satan, his demons and human agents!

You see, dear friends, if you are on God's side there is really no contest – and only time separates the war efforts of the devil and his total annihilation…he, along with his demons

---
42 Mail; snail mail.

and followers will die an **<u>eternal death</u>**. If you are not yet on Jesus' team – get on board! If you already are on board – stay on! Hold on tight…and ***keep the faith***! Jesus is coming soon – **victory for Jesus** is a foregone conclusion!

Heads up soldier! To battle! It – will – soon – be – over!!!

In the meantime, let's consider some weaponry that will definitely give us the edge over the forces of evil! Read on.

The Little Armageddon

Salvation is the issue.
Many will be eternally lost, going headlong into hell while thinking that they are going straight into heaven! This is therefore an extremely serious issue! No one can afford to be wrong on this issue. Remember, we are caught up in a **war** – and the Little Armageddon is an intense battle; and the battle is for the mind! Let us stick to the task. Let us not lose our first love. We cannot afford not to act in this conflict. There is ***no middle ground***.

In this conflict in which we are ***all involved*** it is very crucial to win battles…but it is infinitely more important to win the war! Jesus is the head of the army of truth followers. He is the Archangel, Michael. He is the winner. He already defeated the enemy (Satan) at the cross. We just need to stay on Jesus' side – by ***constantly choosing Him as our Savior and Lord***.

Proverbs 16:25 (Proverbs 14:12) / Matthew 7:21

Chapter Ten

How to Develop Superior Counteracting Weapons for the Little Armageddon

(A Further Look at The Strategies of the Shepherd's Rods: Some Possible Prescriptions for the Church)

Another Favourite Target

Apart from disgruntled members, Shepherd's Rods target teenagers and young people because they are like fertile ground, ***susceptible to new ideas***; they are usually exploring and crave to be "new and different". Shepherd's Rods also target those that are ***not firmly grounded*** or steeped in the Word of God.

<u>**Rx 1:**</u> *Get the young people to **study God's words**! Get them **involved in the work of the Church**! Plan solid, educational and doctrinal programs! Target teenagers and young adults when planning programs and events!* Parents, study with them the fundamental beliefs and the Sabbath School Quarterlies at home during worship, et cetera.

"None but those who have fortified the mind with the truths of the Bible will stand through the last great conflict." GC Chap. 37: The Scriptures a Safeguard, p. 594

New Convert Preparation

Of course, new converts are their favorite targets as they delight in "gobbling them up" - like they would a succulent meal or a luscious fruit or tidbit!

Rx 2: This means that church leaders and pastors had better **WAKE UP!** And really get people ready for baptism and commitment to Jesus! We need to prepare new converts that will really administer some "shock and awe" to some of these Shepherd's Rods! Let them approach a new convert and be so frightened by their quick wit, knowledge, awareness and astute handling of the Word of God that they *literally* run! Hallelujah!!!

Rx 3: Secondarily, Leaders in the church need to make a *deliberate effort* to make the baptismal candidates aware that these offshoots exist and the strategies they use; let the new converts know that the Shepherd's Rods are dangerous!

Let us not give the Shepherd's Rods the benefit of the element of surprise – which is an extremely effective strategy utilized in every kind of warfare! That's a strategy that Satan is using in the Little Armageddon and also in the wider *Great Controversy*. There is a **WAR** going on! Brothers and Sisters let us *never forget that*! Let us not be deceived. **WAKE UP!**

The Need for Nurturing Churches

Rx 4: Our churches need to be so nurturing that provision is made for our young people to be *fully occupied* in ways that *enable them to become very strong spiritually.* In other words, our youth and our new converts should be spiritual giants!

Rx 5: Since the Shepherd's Rods also target other groups and individuals in the Church: Leaders should ensure that the Church is a studying Church – and sermons must be of a nature that will really feed the Church spiritually. We just cannot afford to be just ordinary! Sufficient preparation is key and messages must be biblically based and focused on Jesus.

Other Ways of Attack

Apart from inviting members to lunch or accepting invitations from unsuspecting members and hoping to go undetected in large churches and at Conference and District Conventions, et cetera, Shepherd's Rods attack Church members through other means.

Let me put the question that you are most likely asking right now… "How?"

Well, for example: They will find out telephone numbers and addresses of members and will make calls or visits to their homes OR send literature to them in the mail[43]. Some Adventists have fallen for this, thinking that the literature is coming from a Seventh-day Adventist source.

Members and Leaders Must Be Diligent

Rx 6: This just means that Church Leaders have to be careful and really diligent but must also do something else about it. The entire burden - of course – is not on the leaders; every member must be diligent; every member must work out his or her salvation with fear and trembling! Every member must assist in guarding the flock from the attacks of the Shepherd's Rods.

---

43 The Author has received several of those over the years! I can't be sure where they got my name and address – but I suspect from the telephone directory.

The Little Armageddon

Provide Good Materials For Members to Study!

<u>Rx 7:</u> Churches and Leaders must find ways and means to supply Church members with enough good materials on the doctrines of the church, etc. Frankly, not everyone can afford to buy a copy of the *Fundamental* Beliefs and other such works. Churches could set up **libraries, reading clubs**, or some other type of book-lending program – as a means of filling the need of members to really get the right materials and tools to dig deep into the Word! Along with this must be the means of motivating the membership of the church – young, old and in-between - to study the word of God. There are so many sources of good information available within the Adventist Church! Please, brother and Sisters, use them up – and let others know where and how to access them.

Examples of electronic sources of good tools and materials for studying the word of God as well as witnessing include:

A good website is: www.adventist.org. For good measure one could also go to www.sabbathtruth.com, or www.amazingfacts.org, or www.itiswritten.org or www.voiceofprophecy.org or www.laymenministries.org or http://battlecryministry.netadvent.org

Another very great source of some real Seventh-day Adventist teachings is the Three Angels Broadcasting Network (3ABN) Television; 3ABN also has a website at www.3abn.org where one can view the programs. Also, all the programs are taped and can be obtained from 3ABN usually for a very reasonable contribution. All the Ministries that own the websites mentioned also have an abundance of resources (books, tapes, DVD's, etc.) on a wide variety of topics; while most are for sale some can be obtained free of cost –

through free offers, and so on. Some of the materials on the websites are very valuable and well researched and can be easily downloaded. A search can usually be done by typing in any topic in the search facility provided on the website.

Of course, the local Adventist Book Center usually has an abundance of safe materials available on many, many different topics.

Members who are resource – rich must share and help to support others who are not. This is especially desired and expected of leaders.

Some materials are better shared in the Church in settings where most or all members are present; this will facilitate having as much persons as possible benefiting.

Rx 8: Church programs should be carefully planned to include educating the church on doctrines, and generally to edify the church. Of course, Jesus must always be highly exalted in every teaching or doctrine. All the Leaders in the church must study the Bible and the general membership must be encouraged to study it also. The Leaders must lead by example. The Spirit of Prophecy Writings must also be a part of the Church's regular reading and study.

The Lure of Economic Gain

The next strategy of the Shepherd's Rods that will be mentioned here has been successful with some members of the Church because they have been, plainly, tricked; however, also because some had not learned to really trust God. In other words some go in "with their eyes wide open" while others are caught napping. Some are "caught" because they do not really care how they "get ahead" or are just plain gullible (easily duped). By now you might be able to

The Little Armageddon

guess that it is: <u>Offering economic assistance to members;</u> whether it is an offer to pay school fees or otherwise help with schooling, or the offer of a good job, it is one strategy that is used with some success. This strategy might reap success where members are generally poor and jobless and are genuinely in need of help. This strategy is not unique to the Shepherd's Rods (as are others of their strategies).

Be Our Brothers' Keeper

Rx 9: In the face of the economic lure, what are leaders and members to do? Without going into a lengthy discourse it should suffice to point out that the simple solution is to be our brothers' keeper. We need to really live like the Church is just one big family. Isn't that how it should be? That's certainly how it was in the early (Apostolic) church! So, the remnant church must resemble or be like the original, pure church (Acts 4:32).

Share Problems

We must also develop a genuine culture of sharing our problems in our churches. Those members that are in need must tell somebody; be less secretive if at all – learn to trust others; there is always somebody in church that you can share things with in confidence – find that one; be less proud; also, the members that have much have to be more caring and sharing; they must also be trustworthy; each must be sensitive to the needs of the other. Finally, the department of the church that is assigned the task of caring for he needy must step up to the plate – and start doing its job!

The True Remnant

Dear Reader, what you are about to read might be hard and maybe even absolutely shocking BUT remember, ***the Remnant Church must be exactly like the Apostolic Church.*** In other words, the last piece of cloth must be exactly like the original roll from which it was taken! (See Acts 4:32 – 37). So, no genuine Seventh-day Adventist Christian member of any of our churches should be susceptible to this strategy of economic lure! **Every member can and should be taken care of.**

Psychological Warfare!

One other key strategy that is used by the Shepherd's Rod, particularly against the Church Leadership is a kind of "psychological warfare" (satan pulls out all the stops and pulls no punches; he is a vicious and relentless foe!): They sometimes appear to be very humble and pious, act very calm and gentle and just "full of love". If, as a Leader, you even raise the volume of your voice while speaking to them they will then point out how you are talking loudly and getting upset and that you are just "out of control"; they will argue that you do not have "the right spirit" (in contrast to their "meek" spirit). Their aim is to make the Leader feel guilty, that he / she is doing something wrong to be rebuking them or even speaking to them; they want you to feel that you have sinned / have no right to be speaking out against them; they seek to portray themselves as the ones that are being attacked / unfairly treated (wolves in sheep's clothing!). This is just another way of trying to intimidate the Leader.

Dear Reader, this strategy can be very effective and will work against you if you are caught off-guard. It can be very

The Little Armageddon

devastating! It is like a stealth missile! This sound simple enough but the greater danger is, if they succeed with this strategy it could result in them gaining the sympathies of the members of the Church that are not aware of them, their strategies and the dangers they pose. This could have very serious negative repercussions[44]. You could find yourself faced with serious opposition from members! Even worse, you could witness the breakup of your church!

Hence, one must be *very vigilant* if they use this strategy. Questions may be raised in the minds of some members. Some might wonder: What wrong could these simple-looking, humble people be guilty of? To deserve such (harsh) treatment? Remember, they are usually dressed for this – very conservative, black and white clothing, hat, and so on. In other words – they usually "look the part". So, in your dealings with them try to **remain as calm as possible** (If at all possible); this may be difficult, especially for those of us who know how dangerous this group is; in our anxiety to "get them out" we are in danger of *playing into their hand!* The situation is particularly potentially explosive, ***especially if it is an initial or early encounter.*** Why? Because the Church members might not yet be aware or knowledgeable of them; this lack of knowledge could cause problems.

Rx 10: In this case the best thing to do is to be aware of what the enemy is trying to do. Ensure that you get your confidence level up and also that you ensure that you be very careful how you proceed in this issue. In this case you need to be as wise as a serpent.

---

44   A classical, successful battle strategy - divide and conquer! Get the members to be against the leader! Divide the group – it's easier to destroy it that way.

Witnessing: An Absolute Necessity

Rx 11: One of the most powerful weapons against the Shepherd's Rod attack is to get involved in personal witnessing and in the support of the work of spreading the gospel by supporting it with your means! Get up and start sharing the good news of salvation. It is imperative! It is one of God's commands to us. As members of the Remnant Church we have no option but to obey. Jesus was very clear when He said "Go ye therefore…" (See Matthew 28:18 – 20). As you are led by the Holy Spirit in witnessing for the Lord you will be increasingly grounded in the truth. The doctrines of the church will become clearer and clearer to you as you labour to save souls. As you sacrifice for the cause of God and continue to depend on Him for spiritual guidance and material blessings you will be virtually inoculated from satan's diseases! Satan's miasmas include spiritual lethargy, self indulgence, disobedience, and a whole lot more.

You might do well to consider the following quotes:
"Men are tempted to use their means in self-indulgence, in the gratification of appetite, in personal adornment, or in the embellishment of their homes. For these objects many church members do not hesitate to spend freely and even extravagantly. But when asked to give to the Lord's treasury, to carry forward His work in the earth, they demur. Perhaps, feeling that they cannot well do otherwise, they dole out a sum far smaller than they often spend for needless indulgence. They manifest no real love for Christ's service, no earnest interest in the salvation of souls. What marvel that the Christian life of such ones is but a dwarfed, sickly existence!" {AA 338.2}

"Many, who think that though they are doing no actual work for Christ, they are yet on His side, are enabling the

The Little Armageddon

enemy to pre-occupy ground and gain advantages. By their failure to be diligent workers for the Master, by leaving duties undone and words unspoken, they have allowed Satan to gain control of souls who might have been won for Christ." {COL 280.1}

"We can never be saved in indolence and inactivity. There is no such thing as a truly converted person living a helpless, useless life. It is not possible for us to drift into heaven. No sluggard can enter there. If we do not strive to gain an entrance into the kingdom, if we do not seek earnestly to learn what constitutes its laws, we are not fitted for a part in it. Those who refuse to co-operate with God on earth would not co-operate with Him in heaven. It would not be safe to take them to heaven." {COL 280.2}

"Let none suppose that they can live a life of selfishness, and then, having served their own interests, enter into the joy of their Lord. In the joy of unselfish love they could not participate. They would not be fitted for the heavenly courts." {COL 364.2}

"In the great judgment day those who have not worked for Christ, those who have drifted along, carrying no responsibility, thinking of themselves, pleasing themselves, will be placed by the Judge of all the earth with those who did evil. They receive the same condemnation." {COL 365.1}

"Many who profess to be Christians neglect the claims of God, and yet they do not feel that in this there is any wrong.

Though they have spent their lives in caring for themselves, they will be as much surprised as was the unfaithful servant in the parable to hear the sentence, "Take the talent from him." {COL 365.2}

"Many who excuse themselves from Christian effort plead their inability for the work. But did God make them so incapable? No, never. This inability has been produced by their own inactivity and perpetuated by their deliberate choice.

The continual misuse of their talents will effectually quench for them the Holy Spirit, which is the only light." {COL 365.3}

Dear friend, I beg of you, start witnessing now; it's for your own good. Dear reluctant mainstream member; please shake off the hold of spiritual lethargy and start witnessing.

Dear Shepherd's Rod offshoot; you should be witnessing to others to get them to accept Jesus as their Saviour and Lord – instead of trying to dupe other members of the Seventh-day Adventist Church to follow your false, unbiblical ideas and beliefs.

Final Rx: PRAYER: The Ultimate Weapon!!

The One to *REMEMBER and* Use Often

The most potent prescription is PRAYER. Brothers and sisters, in this Little Armageddon we need to be really praying and staying in touch with Jesus every step of the way!

(1 Thessalonians 5:17).

"We must *pray more, and talk less.* Iniquity abounds, and the people must be taught not to be satisfied with a form of godliness without the spirit and power. If we are intent upon searching our own hearts, putting away our sins, and correcting our evil tendencies, our souls will not be lifted up unto vanity; we shall be distrustful of ourselves, having an abiding sense that our sufficiency is of God." {1SM 122.2}

No man is safe for a day or an hour or a minute without prayer. Especially should we entreat the Lord for wisdom to understand His word. Here are revealed the wiles of the tempter and the means by which he may be successfully resisted. Satan is an expert in quoting Scripture, placing his own interpretation upon passages, by which he hopes to cause us to stumble. We should study the Bible with humility of heart, never losing sight of our dependence upon God. While we must constantly guard against the devices of Satan, *we should pray in faith continually*: "Lead us not into temptation." {GC 530.2}

The Bee Sting

Yesterday I was stung by a bee! I was there, quite contented weeding flowers in the yard while simultaneously cutting the grass as I went along. It was a good, positive experience with physical and even mental and spiritual benefits to boot (I muse a lot when I am involved in this activity).

I had neglected to put on my glove as I usually did when doing this activity. As I reached under a plant to remove some weeds from around it I felt a sharp, piercing sensation near the tip of my index finger. I was surprised and, did not know what had happened. I initially thought it was a thorn-prick but I quickly dismissed that – no thorn could be under that bush; then I realized it was a bee sting – when I looked at it. I quickly rubbed the finger, stroking in the opposite direction to where the sting entered – then quickly took it out. The pain was not an issue for me as I had been stung by dozens of wasps one day; I could have died and, that day was the "fattest" I had ever been since being an adult – but that's another story.

I found myself being sorry for the little bee because I knew that now that he has stung me he will die! I bemoaned the fact that this little creature's productive life would be cut short because of what just happened. I had been pointedly aware of one aspect of the work of the little creatures as I saw them at times around the plants in the yard, including a pumpkin vine that now has a fair-sized pumpkin; I know that, most likely they had something to do with that pumpkin! It speaks of the goodness and marvel of our Creator! God is absolutely marvelous!

As I showered in the evening it struck me that that experience was an analogy for the Little Armageddon. As I thought about it I realized it was not a perfect analogy but there certainly are parallels and lessons to be drawn.

Applications:
1. I was doing quite fine before I reached under the plant. I was involved in a good, right, productive work – and was reaping the benefits! Satan is subtle and, he usually strikes when we least expect it! As we go along life's journey in our walk with the Lord and as we are faced with the *Little Armageddon* we must remain alert; because satan can sting us - and that might change our situation and status in an instant. Be content with and safe in the truth that you know. If what you know is leading you into a closer and closer walk with Jesus and, ultimately, to Heaven – stick with it!
2. The bee was under the plant, hidden from view; as I pushed my hand under the plant, where it was shadowy and dark – in spite of the great

and abundant light of the sun that was shining all around – I got stung. I got stung because I put my hand where the bee was. We must be careful not to go away to secret, shadowy places with the Shepherd's Rod offshoots! That is where they are most dangerous, when they have you separated from the church and other members of the church! Do not go with them to secret places – because under those secret places there is little or no light! This is rather ironic as the Rods claim that they have "higher light", "new light" or "better light" (depending on which ones you speak to). All the time, there is an abundance of light shining elsewhere, where we can bask in the fullness of true light – and ***truth***!

3. I put my hand under the plant without looking under the plant. Chances are, although under the plant was shadowy I might have seen the bee and avoided him if I looked; if I was going to look under the plant I would have to move away some of the leaves in order to expose to the light the portions below. In the Little Armageddon we need to really *look*. Keep your eyes open and be alert at all times. We must also look into the word of God; as we do so, more and yet more light will be revealed; the true light that will come to us from the Bible will save us from falsehoods that will eventually destroy us.

4. For me the bee sting was a little painful; but, I know that, having stung me the bee would eventually die as a result. On the other hand, I survived the sting. It was just a little more than a pin-prick to me and a little hole in the skin of my finger. I survived – and a little charcoal

ensured that by the following morning there was no swelling and very little or no pain! You know, the Rods are doing a work that is evil, painful and harmful to the church on a whole and to individual members; but, the Church of God ***will not* die!** On the other hand, the work the Rods are doing will inevitably lead to *their* death – *eternal death* – if they do not repent (that's frightening!). Many have been stung by the Rods. Some have survived the encounter as it was like a mere pin-prick; for them, it was survivable and, they escaped the tempter's snare!

5. Remember I mentioned that I neglected to put on my glove? If I had the glove on my hand the sting would be literally swallowed up in the thick material of the glove; there would be no way the sting could reach my finger – no way could the venom get into my system! Let me tell you, if we dare act without the guidance of the Holy Spirit in this matter we are going to be deceived. Remember, the Shepherd's Rod is a group that satan originated and is leading; we are in a ***spiritual warfare***; don't think for one moment that you are smarter than them…that you can go study with them and convince them to come back…always ask yourself: "Am I smarter than satan?" Satan deceived one third of the heavenly angels at the beginning of the Great Controversy – and he deceived the parents of humanity. If we are not careful we will be stung! I am telling you brethren, **if we are not under the unction of the Holy Spirit *we will be deceived*!**

6. For most persons, the sting of a bee is no problem – but not so for others. A bee sting contains

The Little Armageddon

venom. When this venom is injected into your body it can cause allergic reactions that can lead to *death*!

*"Allergic reactions can also be triggered throughout the entire body, rather than in one specific location. Called allergic or anaphylactic shock, this response occurs when many cells throughout the body react simultaneously to an allergen, such as **bee sting venom**. The person may experience hives or welts on the skin, itching all over the body, asthmatic spasms in the lungs, or a sudden drop in blood pressure (see Shock). An additional danger is the possibility of swelling in the throat, tongue, and larynx (voice box), which can close the upper airways and cause fatal choking."* (Microsoft ® Encarta ® 2007. © 1993-2006 Microsoft Corporation. All rights reserved.)

Same venom - different person - deadly results! It takes only one sting for the possibility of death to be present. So, dear reader, it's best to avoid the sting if at all possible; avoid contact with the source of the venom. It is really tragic when someone dies as a result of the venom from a bee sting. The sting becomes fatal only after a process has taken place – with no action being taken (or not quick enough) to counteract the poison and prevent a fatal result. Many persons who have been caught by the Shepherd's Rod poison have not reacted by seeking help; they do not extricate themselves from the situation and go where help can be found; they delay and stubbornly continue on the wrong path until they experience *fatal chocking*! They refuse to go to the Great Physician; they stubbornly refuse His pleadings and offers of assistance – and they end up *dying spiritually*; eventually, they will face annihilation; total separation from God. My heart aches! That's absolutely tragic. No one has to end up in that state. Dear reader, if you are a Shepherd's Rod, ***please***, swallow your pride now – come back to the fold, come back on the platform, come back to Jesus! He is willing and able to get the poison out of your system and ultimately *save you*. Won't you give Him a chance to do so? Today? Just say yes – and give it to Jesus; you - won't - ever - regret - it!

Hallelujah!

Chapter Eleven

The Little Armageddon is not for the Weak or the Inexperienced Soldier of the Cross – Nor for the Fainthearted!

Some General Advice for Members

What is stated here **does not** preclude promptings of the Holy Spirit as to how to deal with particular cases. In other words my brother, my sister, be led by the Spirit of God at all times. Seek His advice and, always ask yourself: What would Jesus do? After all, **He** is the Head of the Church!

List of Don'ts
1. *Do not talk to the Shepherd's Rods* with a view to win an argument with them on Biblical or Spirit of Prophecy matters or to persuade them to come back to the main church. Why? The time spent doing that (which might run into many hours!) could be used more profitably to study God's words, to pray or witness *to those who do not yet know the truth*[45]. **For members who are**

---

[45] Same principle applies when witnessing; don't waste time with green fruits – use that time to reap the many ripe fruits that the Lord has prepared - just waiting to be harvested!

spiritually weak it is strongly advised to just follow the first seven words of this paragraph. Our God is an Awesome God. He can change the most stubborn heart and He is the Just Judge. The Spirit of Prophecy also points out that **some** that came down off **the Platform** to examine its foundation returned. This might have happened when Mrs. Houteff and others disbanded the group, and so on. However, the Author is yet to find one Shepherd's Rod that has come back to the true Remnant Church[46].

The member must consider that it is ***highly likely*** they will not be the one to persuade them to come back! This advice is given here because too many Church members waste too much time talking to the Shepherd's Rods. We must have a redemptive, prayerful attitude towards them (as we should towards any others that have "turned back") but that does not mean we have to spend many hours talking to them. In the Author's experience so far even the efforts of Pastors have been fruitless with these persons (remember, "they are stubborn"?). Pray for them.

2. Don't be fooled by their appearance of meekness.
3. Dear member, **don't assume that you are strong**, that you know more than they do and that you "can handle them". (1 Cor.10:12). There are known cases of Pastors and Elders who felt that way. Today, some of them are, very sad to say, Shepherd's Rods themselves. **<u>WAKE UP!</u>** This needs a stronger word than advice … this is no

---

46 I am not alone in this apparent dearth. However, while investigating for this handbook two persons have indicated to the author that they have heard of persons who have returned.

The Little Armageddon

advice … it's a **warning**! Dear Reader, this is **not** a joke, *we are in a war!* Indeed this is the Little Armageddon! And the battle is boiling hot! It's better to be safe – than sorry.

4. Know the truths that you profess to believe. **Know the truth!** Study the Word of God *diligently*. Drink of the fountain of God's words regularly and obey the Spirit of God that inspired the words. When you really know the truth the counterfeit will be very plain to you … it will literally jump out at you. When you really know the truth and the God that inspired the truth there is no way the counterfeit can hide or abide your scrutiny. **Get to know the living Word!** The experts that deal with money inevitably have to contend with counterfeit notes. These experts **do not** spend their time studying the false money; instead, they study and analyze / examine the very *minutest detail* of the genuine note! Then and only then can they identify those notes that do not meet the standard for the genuine! Even then some counterfeits are so cleverly produced and so skillfully presented that it is still *extremely difficult* to identify them[47]. My bother, my sister, when you know the genuine message and is *guided by the Holy Spirit* you will recognize false teachings *as they appear*. It is not up to your knowledge and experience – it is the work of God! Remember friend, the Holy Spirit might also tell you *not to go* to have any discussions with them!

---

[47] Counterfeits are so cleverly done now that it is no longer wise to depend on human senses, skill and training. Hence, the use of machines to detect counterfeit money is now a virtual necessity. (It always amuses me when the tellers, clerks and cashiers hold up those paper notes to the light.)

> If the Holy Spirit tells you that, please obey; again, I say, listen for the Spirit's instruction and obey it! It is my personal belief that this is the area of ***disobedience*** that has caused many to be caught up in deception! The Holy Spirit tells them not to go but they still do so stubbornly and, in a sense of their own self sufficiency. Remember, Jesus counseled, **"go not forth"** (Matthew 24:26). In this issue it can't do any harm to follow that advice! It is an absolute safeguard from deception. Praise the Lord!!!

Final Marching Orders: A Bitter Pill – but Excellent Medicine!

What more can be said?

In addition to all the above scriptures read Paul's words to Titus (Titus 1 verse 9 to Titus 2 verse 1). Having read that, consider the following:

A rather honest ad for a very popular linctus says: "Tastes awful! But it works!"

By their words and actions, sad to say, the Shepherd's Rods are ***hypocrites*** (charlatans, frauds, imposters!). In other words, they pretend to be what they are not. Perhaps Jesus' way of dealing with the hypocrites of His day may be instructive to us as we try to deal with the hypocrites of our day. The following reflection is not for the faint of heart but it is necessary medicine for some who might still think that the church has dealt too harshly with these pretenders or hypocrites:

Read very carefully the following texts: Matthew 7:5; 15:3 – 14; 22:18 – 22; 23:11 – 39; 24:48 – 51; Mark 7:6 – 13;

Luke 11:42 – 52; 12:54 – 59; 13:12 – 17. So, we come to the acid end ... this might seem hard and cutting ... but it needs to be said:

Shepherd's Rods are hypocrites, hypocrites are pretenders, and pretenders are really liars. Why is this being leveled against them? The answer is very plain. Shepherd's Rods teach much falsehood and are proud of what they teach. What are falsehoods (false teachings)? Falsehoods are ***lies***. In other words ***they love to speak and teach lies***. Ananias and Sapphira were pretenders or liars. What happened to them? (Read Acts 5:1 – 11) The further question is what will ultimately happen to all unrepentant liars? (Read Rev. 22:15) Liars will be <u>outside</u> of the Kingdom of God! What I have stated here does not cover everything on this aspect. However, it should be sufficient.

This manual is written for a redemptive purpose as it seeks to warn the church of a deceptive and insidious group that is seeking to draw members out of the church. Members that are drawn away from the Church through any means are in danger of hellfire... because the Church is the gateway to Heaven.

Parting Salvo!

Growing up was not easy; there was often real hardship and a lot of hunger. Going to the neighborhood shop to purchase items was a regular feature of those years. Sometimes the shop was pretty nearby but sometimes it was rather far away. Sometimes a list of items to buy would be written and given to me. Other times there was no written list and each item had to be committed to memory. Sometimes mother would send me off to the shop but after some time passed she would shout for me to return ... she had forgotten to tell me just one more item (sometimes this would even happen more than once in a single instance). It was pretty frustrating to me whenever that happened because as a child going to the shop was not really the fun thing to do; so, it needed to be done quickly, so the other things that are *fun* can be pursued. Moreover, the call to go to the shop usually came when I was having what mattered - fun! But, sometimes the additional item was something that was *really good*; something that I really enjoyed eating ... those were the only times it was really worth the retraced steps!

It is hoped that the following paragraphs will contain something that will make you experience something akin to what I did in the illustration above[48].

I assisted in conducting a Week of Prayer that was a real blessing! The presentation that I was asked to present was that for the second Sabbath and was entitled: "United in the Fellowship of Bible Study". At the time, the topic was unknown to me. It turned out that it had some pertinent statements that directly address the Little Armageddon:

> "Men entertain errors, when the truth is clearly marked out, and if they would but bring their doctrines to the Word of God, and not read the Word of God in light of their doctrines, to prove their ideas right, they would not walk in darkness and blindness, or cherish error".

> "As long as we hold to our own ideas and opinions with determined persistency, we cannot have the unity for which Christ prayed."

---

[48] After thinking that the book was complete the Holy Spirit impressed me that I needed to include these excerpts. May you be blessed as I was as you read them.

"It will not do merely to read God's Word; for the truth it contains is like treasure hid in a field; it does not lie on the surface, and only the earnest, persevering searcher is rewarded by finding the jewels of priceless worth – the inexhaustible riches of Christ Jesus".

"Temptations often appear irresistible because, through neglect of prayer and the study of the Bible, the tempted one cannot readily remember God's promises and meet Satan with the scripture weapons".

Article by Ellen G. White
Adventist Review
Inter-American Edition
October, 2004

"Weird offshoots are nothing new to Adventism. In the early days the denomination was assaulted by a number of strange ideas ranging from pantheism to the "holy flesh" movement." "Ellen White **confronted these threats directly** throughout her writings"

"… she specifically described how cultic error can take over: 'How do men fall into such error? By starting with false premises, and then bringing everything to bear to prove the error true'."

"In some cases the first principles have a measure of truth interwoven with the error, but it does not lead to any just action, and this is why men are misled"

"In order to reign and become a power, they employ Satan's methods to justify their own principles."

> "They exalt themselves as men of superior judgment, and they have stood as representatives of God. These are false gods."

Little Armageddon no More!!!

In stark contrast to **the true Remnant Church of God** that is a Spirit-filled movement that is growing at a truly ***fantastic rate*** (Worldwide, approximately 11 new churches are needed every single day!), the Shepherd's Rods Groups are struggling to survive, ***preying*** on the unsuspecting members of the Church (and those that think they are able to stand and contend with them). The Shepherd's Rod groups are like parasites to the Seventh-day Adventist Church.

While the Shepherd's Rods Groups keep splintering **the Remnant Church of God** is uniting more and more and carrying God's last day message to the world, as Jesus continues His work of perfection in her!

While the Shepherd's Rods groups are ***built upon lies***[49], **the Remnant Church** is built on a firm foundation of solid Bible Truth and on the one who is "...the way, the truth and the life." (John 14:6)

While the original leaders of the Shepherd's Rod Groups declared them to have been <u>**in error**</u> and disbanded, the Seventh-day Adventist Movement keeps moving, steamrolling the kingdom of satan under the banner of Prince Immanuel – in the army of Michael the Archangel!! Hallelujah!!

---

49 Listen, if you mix truth with error you are just like satan – and satan is your dad! So, it matters not if you say "we believe much of what the Seventh-day Adventist Church teach"; you still will be going to the same place satan is going – the place prepared for him and his demons (Matthew 25:41). Please, repent NOW before it's too late (I beg you).

The Little Armageddon

I tell you **the Remnant Church of God** will <u>**never go down**</u>. **The devil cannot win**! The Remnant Church must triumph, for Jesus our High Priest is in Heaven!

We will triumph because **He defeated satan!** Let us get on the winning team! Soon and **very soon Jesus will put an end to the war!** Soon and very soon there will be no more Little Armageddon! Praise the Lord! Soon and very soon there will be **Great Controversy no more! HALLELUJAH!!!**

Dear Reader, I am not a Bible Scholar, a Theologian, a Pastor nor a Doctor (at least, not yet!). I am just a simple Lay Minister. God laid this work on my heart. As long as it was not done I could not find rest. God kept it in my mind.

My brothers and sisters, I now thank God! I have done what I was told, I have, by God's grace, sounded a trumpet … I have tried to be a faithful watchman in Israel[50]. *My conscience is now purged!* Hallelujah!! I hope the trumpet sound is loud enough and will remain long enough that it will reach to the length and bredth of Zion. More importantly, it is hoped that the leaders and members in Zion will make an appropriate response. **It is my personal hope that many Shepherd's Rods will renounce their ways and return as a part of the Remnant Church** – the Church that God will use to finish the work of carrying the gospel to all the world; **the Church that <u>will be</u> victorious!!!**

The Last Thing

One *<u>last</u>* thing: Just in case you have read this book and you believe that you are going to be saved because you have a good "head knowledge" of the doctrines of the church and therefore are able to withstand falsehoods and offshoots; if you believe that as a result of your knowledge and high

---
50 See Ezekiel 33:2 – 6.

intelligence you are "better than them" and, therefore, you must be saved; if you think you will overcome in the final event because you are bright and knowledgeable and a preacher, a teacher or whatever - ***you are absolutely mistaken!*** Our eternal salvation hinges on whether or not we have a living, active, knowing relationship with Jesus Christ and whether or not we have lived in His presence and showed in our choices and actions that He is indeed our Saviour and Lord! It is only when we are fully controlled by the Holy Spirit and ***dead to self*** that we can reach that level in our Christian experience. Never forget that.

May the Lord bless us as we continue to allow Him to use us to accomplish a work in His Vineyard. What a wonderful God! And what a privilege we have to serve Him!!

My, conscience, is, purged.

PRAISE THE LORD!!!

My Final Appeal

I would like to use this opportunity to appeal to those who are currently a part of a Shepherd's Rod group to reconsider their position and get back on the ship of Zion. Get back on the platform of the Word of God. Get back in the Seventh-day Adventist Church as full-fledged members.

Jesus is coming soon and anyone who does not find themselves within the ambit of His Church, His Bride that He is going to return to get, will be truly left behind. Jesus is the one coming for His bride. We need to be married to Jesus as individuals and only a genuine close, personal relationship with Jesus will save us. If we have that relationship and we truly love Jesus we will be a part of His church, His body, His bride.

The Little Armageddon

Sometimes we get caught up in something and then get too comfortable in it – even after we find out it's not right and proper to be in (like a frog being slow-cooked!); other times the problem is our **pride**. Please let go of the falsehoods and hold on to the truth of the Gospel of Christ. No one can afford to risk his or her soul's salvation because of concern of what some other person might think of or say about them. We are talking about eternal life or eternal separation from God here!

If you became a Shepherd's Rod because you were hurt by someone in the Church let me express how sorry I am and ask that you forgive us. God offers us His forgiveness fully and freely. Please forgive as Jesus would, get back in and get ready for Jesus' second coming. Absolutely nothing; no problem is too big for the Lord to handle – and there is ***absolutely nothing*** that we should let keep us from living with and worshipping God *forever*.

I can assure you that if you take but one step towards Jesus, if you study His life and work and seek to follow Him – you will be filled with joy that you did! Because Jesus will take you and give you the victory you need from the vice grip of false teaching that is binding you.

Satan is a liar and a deceiver and he wants you – he wants all of us to be lost. On the other hand, Jesus loves us with a ***supreme, everlasting love.*** He desires that **all of us** be saved. If you or I do not make the right choices and end up missing out on Heaven then all that we do now in word or deed, in work or worship, will be utterly useless and wasted.

If you spend your time and effort in doing a work that is not sanctioned by God you will be lost – but it wont and cannot be God's fault. God has done everything possible for you and I to be saved – we need to choose to follow Him who is ***the way, the truth and the life*!**

On that great and **awesome day** it will be too late; on that day when all the hosts of Heaven and earth are all together, spread out like two ginormous seas separated by an awful gulf of separation – separation caused by unforgiveness, by anger, by selfishness, by stubbornness… by ***sin*;** the one sea composed of the redeemed of all ages who had washed their robes and made them white in the blood of The Lamb and followed Him wherever He went – the other made up of those who chose not to follow the Lamb.

What – a – day – that – will – be!

Where will you be? Where will I be? Which sea will you be a part of?

I want to be a part of the sea of redeemed!

I choose by God's grace to accept and serve Him both now and forever.

Won't you join me in this choice?

Absolutely nothing else matters!!
Absolutely nothing else is more important than our souls' salvation!!!

If we do not meet here on earth in these momentous closing scenes of the Great Controversy, I hope and trust that I will see you in the Kingdom of Heaven!

HALLELUJAH!!!

MARANATHA!!!

www.ingramcontent.com/pod-product-compliance
Lightning Source LLC
Chambersburg PA
CBHW032110090426
42743CB00007B/305